SOFTWARE TESTING AS A SERVICE

SOFTWARE TESTING AS A SERVICE

ASHFAQUE AHMED

CRC Press
Taylor & Francis Group
Boca Raton   London   New York

CRC Press is an imprint of the
Taylor & Francis Group, an **informa** business

AN AUERBACH BOOK

CRC Press
Taylor & Francis Group
6000 Broken Sound Parkway NW, Suite 300
Boca Raton, FL 33487-2742

© 2010 by Taylor & Francis Group, LLC
CRC Press is an imprint of Taylor & Francis Group, an Informa business

No claim to original U.S. Government works
Printed in the United States of America on acid-free paper
10 9 8 7 6 5 4 3 2 1

International Standard Book Number-13: 978-1-4200-9956-0 (Softcover)

Library of Congress Cataloging-in-Publication Data

Ahmed, Ashfaque.
  Software testing as a service / Ashfaque Ahmed. -- 1st ed.
    p. cm.
  Includes bibliographical references and index.
  ISBN 978-1-4200-9956-0 (alk. paper)
  1. Computer software--Testing. 2. Computer software industry. I. Title.

  QA76.76.T48A53 2009
  005.1'4--dc22   2009009590

Visit the Taylor & Francis Web site at
http://www.taylorandfrancis.com

and the CRC Press Web site at
http://www.crcpress.com

Contents

Preface

Contrary to the title of the book, *Software Testing as a Service*, we can think of software testing as a manufacturing activity and not as a service. Yet, by doing so we can commoditize the software testing service. This can have tremendous impact on schedules, quality, and cost, and is now possible, because now many service providers can get many software testing projects to work on at the same time. It would not be possible if any service provider does not get many projects to work on simultaneously. The software services provider can set up a centralized organization that can handle all existing and incoming test projects and deliver them using shared resources. Each project is like a manufactured item that is in queue and then, when its turn comes, gets processed using the resources and then delivered. In fact parts of a project (modules, test cases, etc.) can be considered as inventories that need to be queued and then processed. Each such inventory will have three states (i.e., queued, work-in-process, and finished.) As in manufacturing, we can have production lines and processing departments.

Doesn't this look like a utopian idea? Well, it is just short of happening in reality. Many offshore outsourcing service providers have reached the stage of consolidating test projects and using shared resources to deliver these projects and are in fact delivering the goods, saving millions of dollars for their customers. Using this new methodology, we can do and save even more for our customers and yet still deliver with unmatched quality and with a record reduction in schedule.

I had been thinking of writing a book on this subject for some time, as I felt there was a need to take a step forward and think of a way to achieve something that is not possible via traditional functioning. To express this, I have coined a new phrase: *mass servicing*, akin to *mass manufacturing*. It is my belief that we can achieve something similar to what mass manufacturing achieved for the manufacturing sector and for society at large and in the process, we can truly commoditize software testing. Chapter 12 of the book discusses this concept of software testing as a manufacturing activity in detail. Chapter 11 discusses the benefits of offshoring test projects, including even and consistent quality across projects, consolidation of projects, and sharing of resources. Chapter 13 discusses the relationships among quality, standards, and software testing. This is most important because many people get confused regarding the difference between software quality and software testing. This chapter discusses and explains the differences and the relationships between the two. Other chapters discuss project planning, risk management, customer expectation management, project reporting, project execution, and some other aspects of software testing. There are checklists provided in Chapters 3 through 8 that will be very useful for test managers.

Readers of this book will benefit by gaining new ideas about software testing from the perspective of a customer who outsources his project to an outsourcer. However, the book deals more with addressing challenges from the outsourcing partner's perspective and that the software test project is being executed from an offshore location. That is why the title of the book is *Software Testing as a Service*.

Since I have a strong grounding in manufacturing, I have tried to explain many software testing concepts from the manufacturing perspective. This is a new approach for a book written on the subject of software testing management.

Conventions in this book are per the standards specified in the Capability Maturity Model for Integration (CMMI). The time has come for software development and software maintenance and support (after deployment services) to be governed not by separate processes, but rather under a single umbrella. This is the reason all illustrations and concepts in this book follow CMMI standards.

Great effort has been made to explain concepts in an easy-to-understand style using layman's language. Consequently, even beginners will be able to understand these topics. Examples and case studies have also been provided wherever possible to make it easy to grasp these concepts.

A great effort has also been made to discuss only current and relevant topics. This will help readers to get current and useful information.

I strongly believe that the readers of this book will benefit greatly from the information presented within. This is my sole purpose in writing this book. I hope the book will succeed in its intended goal.

Ashfaque Ahmed

Acknowledgments

This book is dedicated to my mother, Aesha, and the kids in the family, Sofia, Arisha, Shija, Ashi, and Jasim. I have always gotten inspiration from my mother, who has supported me in everything I have done in my life. Likewise, the kids have always shown me how to be happy even when life looks to be in dire straits. They are the chirpy little people in my life. I hope someday they will become better writers than I am. I am also indebted to my brother Javed, who has supported me in everything I have done in my life. His contribution has been tremendous and has included helping me with the cover design, images, and reviews for this book. My youngest brother, Aslam, has also helped me prepare material for this book.

In my professional life (spanning more than 20 years now) I have come across some wonderful people from whom I learned how to be successful. I am thankful to all of them. In particular, I am especially thankful to Gary Hahn of One Network Enterprises, who has been a wonderful manager and a caring human being, and has also contributed by reviewing this book. I am also thankful to my colleague Dinesh Salvi, who reviewed the book, as well as all my colleagues at Entercoms Software Private Limited with whom I shared unforgettable moments while working on our assignments.

In my personal life I have met influential people whose perspective helped me to understand many aspects of my life better. One such person is Nandu Phadke, a distinguished lawyer and a person with great integrity.

I am also thankful to my publisher, Auerbach Publications, who gave me the opportunity to write this book.

About the Author

Ashfaque Ahmed is a consultant for software testing and supply chain management. He has over 20 years of experience in the software industry and has served clients with innovative solutions that have saved millions of dollars. He has worked with both midsize and large multinational customers on engagements involving implementing and testing enterprise software applications. The industries served included manufacturing, retail, distribution, and transportation. He also has worked on product development for a midsize enterprise software vendor.

Over the years Mr. Ahmed has written many research papers that were published by Technology Evaluation Centers Inc. (http://www. technologyevaluation.com).

Recently Ahmed started SCM Consulting (http://www.scmconsultingonline. com), a portal that provides valuable information to students and software professionals on areas covering software testing, implementation, development, and selection.

Ahmed holds a bachelor's degree in engineering and an MBA in information systems and is also a Microsoft Certified Professional.

Chapter 1

Introduction to Software Testing Management

Believe me, software testing management is one of the most difficult tasks out there. There are many reasons for this. First, a software product is not a tangible thing that can be measured, physically felt, or sampled. So it is difficult to test a software product. Second, software testing is still not considered a recognized trade and so finding professionally qualified people for the testing job is difficult. Third, unlike well-defined and standardized processes for product design, product development, quality control, and so on, which exist for any product development activity, similar standardized processes have yet to be defined for software testing. Fourth, tools for automation of software testing activities are still in their nascent stage, and it will take time to have sophisticated automation tools available for software testing activities. Fifth, effort estimation techniques for software testing activities are still being evolved, and currently effort estimation is done mostly on an ad hoc basis.

Yet, the importance of software testing is so immense! Any failure of the software product or application can cause damages to the tune of millions of dollars for any company. Even if the software defect is not so big, the support cost can run in the thousands of dollars over the life of the software product.

To better understand software testing management, let us first try to understand what is a defect in a product, how it affects a user, what the user feels when he finds a defect in a product after buying and using it, how to prevent defects, and finally how to identify and remove defects in the physical world. Then from there we can go to software engineering and software testing. From there we can move on to software testing management aspects.

1

1.1 Product Defect: A Case Study

Just the other day I bought a semi-automatic washing machine. It had a 2-year warranty on it, and the deal looked fine. So I bought it. My wife started using it, and everything looked fine till one day. That day my wife phoned me saying the washing machine is not working. I was in the midst of an office meeting. I was deeply involved in my task at hand and I got disturbed. Now my wife is very blunt when it comes to talking on the phone and when she says something to me, it is a command and not a request. I must do something immediately or else I face the risk of being called an incompetent person. Even if I am busy with something important, I must obey. Cursing my wife and the washing machine company, I told my wife to find the customer service phone number of the washing machine company from the product brochure that came with the washing machine and get it fixed. I also told my wife not to disturb me, as she can handle these things herself. When I came back home that day, I learned that the mechanic had found something stuck in the drainage system of the washing machine and the mechanic cleaned and fixed it. A few days later, my wife phoned me, saying that the washing machine again has some problem. I told my wife not to bother me, as she has the customer service phone number of the washing machine company and she can phone them directly. So my wife phoned the washing machine company and got the machine fixed. This happened many times over the next few months. Finally I decided to confront the service engineer myself and tried to get an explanation as to why it was happening. I found out that that particular brand of washing machine had a design problem and this problem was happening with most of the washing machines of that brand. I talked to customer service and explained my problem. Even after a lot of heated exchanges I was not able to find a solution from the company. Then I thought I should look inside the washing machine and find out the problem myself. So here I was disassembling the washing machine and trying to find out the root cause of the problem. I found out that there was a valve (to stop or start draining of water from the washing machine) connected to the drainage system of the machine and the valve used to activate when a lever attached to the machine was pushed. Dirt coming out of the clothes was getting deposited at the valve and clogging it. So the valve was not closing properly and water was getting drained even when the valve was in the closed position. Water should not come out when clothes are being washed. When washing is complete, you can open the valve to let the dirty water out of the washing machine by pressing the valve lever. I cleaned the valve and then tested it by filling water in the washing machine. I inspected the valve and the lever to find out the problem. I found out that even when the valve was clean the lever was not properly closing the valve and so the valve was getting only half closed. This was the root cause of the problem. I also found out that there was no option to adjust the lever so that it should be able to close the valve completely when operated. So far I was able to trace the root cause of the problem. Now I had to fix it. After thinking much, I decided to bend a part of the lever so that the length of the lever would get changed and so it can push the valve more and close it more. After some trial and error I was able to make the lever pull the valve perfectly. So the valve was getting opened properly now, but still the valve was not getting closed properly. To this day this problem could not be fixed even after many attempts by service engineers.

1.2 Case Analysis

What is the moral of the story? A small defect in a part of a product can dent confidence of the customers. I for sure will never buy any products from the manufacturer who manufactured that godforsaken washing machine.

This shows the importance of preventing defects in the first place and, if any defect occurs, finding it at the manufacturing site itself and removing that defect so that the defect is not passed to end users or customers.

Preventing as many defects as possible in the product and then trapping defects if any occur at the manufacturing site itself is very important. Right from product conception to product design to production, a process should be followed which will ensure that the product is as close to defect-free as possible. This means that when a machine prototype is passed to the machine design team, the machine prototyping team should ensure that no defects are introduced in the prototyping. When machines made from this design are then installed at the shop floor, the factory should ensure that no defects are passed to the product being made on this machine due to faulty material handling or bad machine design. These measures will ensure defect-free products through a thorough implementation of quality assurance processes. Similarly the product that will be produced using this machine should also go through the same quality assurance process at each stage of product conception to product design to product production. And at each stage in the manufacturing process the quality testing department should ensure that any defects which may occur in the product are trapped and faulty products are either reworked or rejected.

In the physical world preventing and removing defects is very much possible to the extent of having products 99.99999% defect-free. It is possible because a number of factors that cause defects can be determined and then removed from design or during the manufacturing process. Nowadays product development has matured so much that in most of the industries defects due to faulty conception and design are nonexistent. They have also mastered manufacturing processes so that they can achieve defect-free products to the tune of 99.99999%. They have feverishly implemented six sigma programs, ISO standards, lean manufacturing principles, quality circle programs, and so on. So the first principle is that defects should not be introduced in the products. The second principle is that if some defects enter at any stage, then they should be trapped before the product enters into the next stage in the production cycle. One good example of this trend is the introduction of Toyota's manufacturing system. At Toyota Motors the quality processes are so strong that their cars are virtually defect-free. This has helped Toyota tremendously in capturing market share and reducing their manufacturing costs. The Toyota manufacturing model has become a de facto standard in the automobile industry, and subsequently other industries have followed their example.

1.3 Return on Investment

From another point of view, preventing defects as early as possible presents a compelling ROI perspective. Say cost of finding and fixing a defect at prototype stage is US$40. This defect is not found and is passed on to the design stage, where it is trapped and fixed. In that case the cost of fixing it would be at least fivefold as the defective prototype has gone into design and so design is also flawed and needs to be fixed as well. At the same time this one prototype defect introduces five design defects. After the production stage this cost will become at least 25-fold from the prototype, as now either the product prototype along with the machine design will also have to be fixed or these 25 defects after the design stage have to be fixed. Finally, when it comes to customer site, the cost will be a staggering 125 times that of the prototype stage, as now support cost will also get involved. So the cost of fixing the defect will be US$5000 ($40 × 125). So you see it definitely makes sense to fix the defect as early as possible. Of course, time and cost constraints put a limit on to what extent defects should be traced and fixed. But continuous improvement techniques help to reduce defect injection and improve defect prevention over a period of time once the techniques are introduced. This is what CMM (Capability Maturity Model) talks about.

Coming to a software product, suppose for each quarterly release on average 500 must-fix defects are found. The cost of fixing each defect at build phase is at $100; at testing phase, $500; and at customer end, $2500. Now suppose the software vendor has no testers. Industry standard is that 25% of errors are detected by developers, 50% on average by skilled testers, and the remaining 25% by end users. In our case, because no testers are involved, 75% of total defects are detected and fixed at customer site after 25% of defects are detected and fixed by developers. Total cost of fixing defects comes to $887,500 ($12,500 + $875,000).

Now suppose we employed three software testers at $50 per hour. So their total salary for the quarter comes to $108,000. In this scenario the cost of fixing defects comes to $495,500 ($12,500 + $108,000 + $375,000).

Compared to the previous scenario we can see that we are saving $392,000. This is a saving of more than 44% over the case when no testers are deployed. So it can be clearly seen that there is a great return on investment (ROI). The ROI improves further when the testing function is outsourced and even further when it is offshored.

In Chapter 11, we introduce a new concept of commoditizing software testing service. If this concept can be devised, refined, and finally implemented, it can provide tremendous cost savings to customers.

1.4 Causes of Defects in Software

But why does the software industry still find it difficult to produce defect-free software? Well, there are many reasons for it. Software does not have a physical form that can be seen, and defects can be found during conception, design, or build. The factors that can induce defects in the software products are too numerous to list here. For instance, all the internal and external parts of the software are made up of small parts of software or, in other words, a set of instructions. Internal defects are bound to exist in some of these thousands of sets of instructions inside a big software product so that at the complete software level the number of defects could run in the thousands. There is one more source of defects apart from internal defects. Software is made up of modules, and modules are made up of submodules. These modules and submodules are integrated with each other through their interfaces. Even if the data gets passed through these interfaces during transaction execution, it is not the right data passing through these interfaces. For example, suppose there is a module for product master list and product names are being fetched using this module from other modules. This is done through a mechanism of product code lists that are matched in both modules (product master module and the other module that wants to display product names). Due to the mismatching of product list, it is possible that wrong product names are being displayed. Thus we have a genuine functional error here.

Now let us see a list of causes that introduce defects in software:

- **Miscommunication or no communication**—Software specification or requirements are not understood by the project team due to miscommunication or no communication among the project team.
- **Software complexity**—Software applications are getting more complex due to an increase in complexity in requirements. This complexity leads to more defects creeping into the software application. Proliferation of many kinds of software applications with diverse technology backbones also leads to complexity of software applications. Multitiered applications, client-server and distributed applications, data communications, enormous relational databases, and the sheer size of applications have all contributed to the exponential growth in software/system complexity.
- **Programming errors**—If design specifications are not understood by programmers or if programmers make mistakes in programming structures or implement any design wrongly by mistake, then defects will be introduced in the software.

■ **Changing requirements**—This is one of the most important sources of defects in software. A change in requirements upsets the whole project, from design to build to testing to deployment. In extreme situations, it may lead to the throwing away of all already designed and built software. In other cases, it may lead to significant change required in existing design and build. Sometimes a small change required in one module of software may lead to significant changes required in other dependent modules. These factors result in the introduction of inadvertently introduced defects in the software.

■ **Overloading of resources**—Due to intangibility and the abstract nature of any software product, it is very difficult to make a good schedule for software projects. This results in bad scheduling, which causes many software professionals to be overloaded. This results in more introductions of defects in the software. Most of the time software professionals find it difficult to meet deadlines, and this results in hasty and less careful work, resulting in more defects in the software.

■ **Less skillful resources**—The software profession needs very skilled and experienced professionals. Many times less skilled professionals are recruited due to lack of skilled professionals in the market. This results in introduction of more defects in the software.

■ **Unprofessional attitude**—Many times professionals on the project have attitude problems. They take their assignments lightly, play office politics, or try to shun their assigned work and off-load it to other members of the team. These tactics not only create problems in meeting deadlines for the project but also result in introduction of more defects in the software.

■ **Poor documentation**—This is another primary source of defects in the software. In the case of smaller projects where some form of extreme programming or agile programming is followed, less documentation is acceptable because the project team is located at one place, and due to smaller software, complexity is less. But in the case of bigger projects where the team may be located at different sites and where software requirements are complex, good documentation is very important. Otherwise, the team runs a great risk of introducing more defects. Another aspect of poor documentation is difficulty in maintaining the software application after it goes into production.

■ **Development tools**—In today's fast-paced business environment, project teams use many tools to increase their productivity. Some of these tools include visual tools, class libraries, compilers, scripting tools, RAD (rapid application development), integrated development studios, integration tools, and so on. Many times these tools introduce their own defects, and sometimes, due to their poor documentation, help in adding defects.

1.5 Factors Creating Problems in Software Development Process

Software development is a very difficult and labor-intensive process. Not many people have software development skills. That is why good software developers are always in great demand. If you are building software application from scratch, then you will need a meticulous plan to define a good process, assemble a good team, provide a detailed idea as to what the software will do, provide details about different functionalities in the application, select appropriate programming language, select appropriate technology and tools, and so on.

Let us see in detail what major problems are encountered by software development teams:

- **Intangibility**—When you develop any physical product, all of the product attributes can be seen and measured. Hypothesis can be done for changes in any product attribute whether it is physical dimensions, colors, chemical composition, and so on, and resulting product attribute changes can be again measured and any abnormal or undesired properties of the product can be observed or measured by creating mathematical models of the product. So testing a physical product is easy. But in the case of software products, you are dealing with intangible products. The only thing you see is the user interface. How the product is conceived, architectured, and implemented remains a mystery. By going through the documentation and code reviews you can find out about these things, but still on a large scale these things are a mystery. This is why software product development is a difficult proposition.
- **Poor requirements**—If requirements are unclear, incomplete, too general, or not testable, then there are bound to be problems in software development. Poor requirements also lead to bad design.
- **Unrealistic schedule**—If too much work is crammed into too little time, problems are inevitable. Loading of resources to an unrealistic level leads to downfall in resource productivity.
- **Inadequate testing**—Without software testing in development, no one will know whether the program is performing as per specifications. All the defects will be found by customers, which is the worst-case scenario.
- **Featuritis**—Like diseases, too many changes in requirements leads to unhealthy software. This is called featuritis. In most software development projects it happens and is a major cause of defective software application.
- **Miscommunication**—Even when customers, the development team and other stakeholders are located nearby and meet frequently and exchange information, miscommunication happens. This leads to wrong expectations and wrong information, and everything about the project gets messed up.

The development team gets wrong requirements and so design becomes faulty and subsequently the coding will be entirely wrong. In today's world of scattered teams located at far-flung geographic locations, communication becomes even more difficult, which leads to more miscommunications.

1.6 Solutions to Software Development Problems

It is easy to get carried away with the common problems that exist with most of the software development projects. Nevertheless it is possible to overcome these problems. Using a well-documented and well-defined process coupled with good planning for the project can ensure successful navigation of these bottlenecks.

Let us take a look at solutions for solving these problems:

- **Solid requirements**—Clear, complete, detailed, cohesive, attainable, and testable requirements do wonders for any project. In agile-type environments, continuous close coordination with customers/end users is required to ensure that changing/emerging requirements are understood by the development team. This is the first step in software development: that requirements should be clear and no ambiguity should exist.
- **Realistic schedules**—Allow adequate time for planning, design, testing, defect fixing, retesting, and changes to be made as per requirements and documentation at each stage including requirements, design, coding, and testing. Without a realistic schedule, team members will be forced to take recourse to make shortcuts, which is detrimental to any project.
- **Adequate testing**—Start testing early on right after getting requirements, always retest after fixes or changes, and plan for adequate time for testing and defect fixing. Testing should include static code analysis/testing, test-first development, unit testing and integration testing by developers, built-in testing and diagnostic capabilities, automated postbuild testing, and so on, apart from the usual performance, system, and acceptance testing that is done after the application is built.
- **Communication**—Communication has always been the most important worry in any project where a team is working to achieve a shared goal. In software projects its importance increases, as software development work is a very specialized form of group work. Any layman will never understand the kind of work being done. Communication among software project team members is thus different in scope and importance. Even after strict adherence to processes and standards set for the project, a communication gap is bound to happen and will impact the project adversely. Some of the communication channels used in software projects include walkthroughs, inspections, knowledge transfer, white boards, and conference calls. The team should make extensive use of group communication tools like groupware, instant

messengers, wikis, defect-tracking tools and change-management tools, intranet capabilities, and so on, to ensure that information/documentation is available and up-to-date. Electronic exchange is preferable, as it is fast and easy to share among team members and end users. Promote teamwork and cooperation; use prototypes and/or continuous communication with end users if possible to clarify expectations.

1.7   Definition of Software Quality

From the perspective of the customer, outsourcer, or any other stakeholder, the definition of software quality may vary. However, on a broader level we can say that good-quality software is reasonably defect-free, is delivered on time and within budget, meets requirements, meets expectations, and is maintainable.

Let us face it: *quality* is a subjective term. So software quality will depend on who the customer is and the customer's involvement in the overall software project. Enterprise software applications are used by many people at the customer organization like customer support people, factory shop personnel, clerks, accountants, and in fact most of the people working for that customer. So here the customer can be defined as the end users, customer acceptance testers, customer contract officers, customer management, the development organization's management, accountants, testers, salespeople, future software maintenance engineers, stockholders, and so on. Each type of customer who will be evaluating the value of the software application will have their own way of defining and measuring quality; for example, the accounting department might define quality in terms of return on investment, while an end user might define quality as user-friendliness and a defect-free product.

1.8   Definition of Good Design

Good software design is the design that incorporates the latest but proven technology, has a scalable structure, facilitates easy integration with other systems, and is flexible to allow incorporating changes in requirements. If the design is built for older technology, then the system might become obsolete too soon. For example, if the design team thinks of using mainframe technology, then it is not appropriate. Similarly if the design team thinks of employing some new unproven technology, then it could be a great risk that the application after development may become obsolete soon as the new technology has failed. Businesses always keep on expanding, and any system deployed should also scale up nicely so that the new needs of the customer are incorporated in the application when they arise in the future. Nowadays there are too many legacy systems for fulfilling different business needs within the customer's premises as well as the application needs to be integrated with customer's suppliers, contractors, customers, and so on. So the application should be easily integratable with these myriad systems. Requirements keep changing very often; this is a fact of life. The design should be flexible enough to take care of these changes in requirements.

1.9 Definition of Good Code

Good code is code that works as intended, is reasonably defect-free, and is readable and maintainable. Most organizations have coding standards that all developers adhere to. Over time, organizations develop a framework that becomes mature and reliable. There are too many methodologies out there, but organizations should stick to what suits them best for their projects. Also excessive use of standards and rules stifle the productivity and creativity of team members. So some room for creativity should be left. In fact software development is such a creative endeavor that no project team can develop any software application just by adhering to processes.

Peer reviews, pair programming, code analysis tools, and so on, can be used to check for problems and enforce standards. For object-oriented programming, here are some typical ideas to consider in setting rules/standards:

- Minimize or eliminate use of global variables.
- Use descriptive function and method names—use both uppercase and lowercase, avoid abbreviations, and use as many characters as necessary to be adequately descriptive. Be consistent in naming conventions.
- Use descriptive variable names—use both uppercase and lowercase, avoid abbreviations, and use as many characters as necessary to be adequately descriptive. Be consistent in naming conventions.
- Function and method sizes should be minimized. Less than 100 lines of code is good; less than 50 lines is preferable.
- Function descriptions should be clearly spelled out in comments preceding a function's code.
- Organize code for readability.
- Use white spaces generously—vertically and horizontally.
- Each line of code should contain 70 characters max.
- One code statement per line.
- Coding style should be consistent throughout a program (e.g., use of brackets, indentations, naming conventions).
- In adding comments, err on the side of too many rather than too few comments; a common rule of thumb is that there should be at least as many lines of comments (including header blocks) as lines of code.

- No matter how small, an application should include documentation of the overall program function and flow or if possible a separate flowchart and detailed program documentation.
- Make extensive use of error-handling procedures and status and error logging.
- To minimize complexity and increase maintainability, avoid too many levels of inheritance in class hierarchies (relative to the size and complexity of the application). Minimize use of multiple inheritances, and minimize use of operator overloading (note that the Java programming language eliminates multiple inheritance and operator overloading).
- Make liberal use of exception handlers.

1.10   Definition of Testing

Before we go into a detailed description of software testing, let us first discuss a small testing example. Suppose you have to test a tea vending machine. How can you do that?

1.10.1   Case Study

The tea vending machine consists of just one tea outlet. There is just one button, which, when pressed, will let the tea come out of the spout.

So there is just one input in this example from the user's perspective: press of the single button.

The outputs in this example from the user's perspective are as follows:

- Does the output taste like tea or something else?
- Is the proper quantity of tea pouring out with one press of the button?
- Is the temperature of the output proper (say, 70°C)?
- Has sugar, milk, or any other additive already been added?

Now take a look at the perspective of the maintenance engineer.

1.10.1.1   Inputs

- Tea powder pouch filling in the machine at fixed intervals.
- Water heating system working properly.
- Internal pipes for tea and additives are working properly, and there is no clogging.
- Sugar/milk powder pouch filling in the machine at fixed intervals.
- Push button is working fine.

- Electricity is working fine.
- Proper mixing of sugar/milk or any other additives in the tea.

1.10.1.2 Outputs

- Does the output taste like tea or something else?
- Is the proper quantity of tea pouring out with one press of the button?
- Is the temperature of the output proper (say, 70°C)?
- Has sugar, milk, or any other additive already been added?

1.10.1.3 Analysis

In the first example we are testing the tea vending machine from the end user perspective. Here the end user is not concerned with the internal working of the machine. He is concerned only with what inputs are to be given to the machine (here pressing the push button) to get the desired output (right quality and quantity of tea). For testing the machine, he inputs the desired and not so desired activity and validates it by getting the quality and quantity of output. The kind of output (valid/invalid) he gets against desired/undesired inputs provides him enough information as to whether the machine is working fine or not.

In software testing a similar kind of activity is carried out, what is popularly known as black box testing. Test engineers are given a software application along with requirements and design documents and are asked to verify whether the application is performing as per expectations mentioned in the requirements and design documents. The test engineer does not care how the application was built. He tests the application only by providing some valid/invalid data and getting the output. By comparing actual output with expected output, he validates whether the application is working fine or not.

In contrast, consider the second example of a maintenance engineer. He is responsible for the proper functioning of the equipment. So he periodically checks the machine by checking the internal working of the machine to ensure that all parts are functional and that the machine as a whole is working fine.

1.10.1.4 Conclusion

In software testing parlance, this kind of testing is known as white box testing. The test engineer knows the internal working of the application. Here the test engineer has the source code or at least open interfaces of the application. He either inserts test code or passes some data through open interfaces to get outputs from the application. By comparing desired outputs against the actual outputs, he validates whether the application is working fine or not.

The internal defect testing is known as unit testing, and it is done by developers themselves. Integration defect testing is known as integration testing, and again it is done by developers. Unit and integration testing is collectively known as white box testing. One more external source of defects is integration with other software systems. In any company at any point in time there are many enterprise systems that are used for different purposes and are integrated to each other. This integration happens at the application or database level. Integration can also be done using middleware software. Nowadays one more type of integration happens. With the proliferation of software service components (known as SAAS or "software as a service"), loosely coupled integration happens between an application and a SAAS component. For example, one travel portal offers cheap airfares to users through their portal. When a user tries to choose the cheapest fares, the portal application sources data available with SAAS components of different airlines and comes up with comparative fares and presents it to the user. All this happens in real time, and the user gets current fare data from many airlines. This kind of functionality is not possible if the portal is tightly coupled with the application.

1.11   Software Testing Evolution

Welcome to the world of software testing! Software testing is not a new field, having existed for over 60 years now. But its importance has been recognized for only the last 10 years or so. Earlier software development processes used to have only one phase for testing. Software used to get designed after getting requirements and then it was developed. Once software was developed, it would be thrown at software testers to test it. Some defects may be found and rectified, and then it was handed over to end users.

Even if end users had problems using this defective software, they were helpless, as their management was happy just to have that piece of software installed at their premises. It was the era when software development guys were the kings and whatever complaints the end users had with the installed software would go to deaf ears. The market conditions were such that there were not many software vendors and software service providers in the market, and so the end users were supposed to accommodate shoddy software without any complaints.

After the Internet started becoming popular in the 1990s, the number of software companies mushroomed. This started a sense of competition among software companies. With competition came price wars, addressing quality of software products, and so on. And due to this change in scenario, rebirth of software testing took place. Also, as the architecture of Internet-enabled software systems or software applications are hugely different from old mainframe or client server applications, software development methodology also got changed. The new software development model, called agile development or extreme programming, has changed many aspects of software project management. This has also made a big impact on software testing. This kind of testing calls for approaches that are well suited for iterative and incremental software testing. Not only does the test team get involved with black box and other kinds of testing, but a major part of their activities also involves regression testing as and when new parts are added to the software product with the existing functionality.

The introduction of the Internet has brought additional new challenges. Because the Web sites and portals are accessible by anybody, security threats pose a great danger. Personal and financial information can be easily stolen. So there is a great need to make these portals and Web sites secure so that information cannot be stolen easily. Security testing plays a great role in ensuring that these software applications are secure.

There are millions of users who throng popular Web sites. Due to this, the servers hosting these Web sites come under heavy load. These heavy loads can take the application server down by exceeding memory capacity or computer processor capacity or crash the computer network due to the huge number of data transfer requirements. Performance and load testing ensures that these problems are not faced by the user community or owners of the Web site. Software engineers perform performance testing to expose the bottlenecks so that necessary changes can be made in the hardware and software to prevent such occurrences.

Many software testing tool providers have made life easier for test engineers. Many tasks that they used to do manually can be automated now with help of these testing tools. So a significant number of software test projects now involve automating testing tasks.

1.12 Software Engineering

To reduce defects in software products, measures have been taken over the years. Software engineering principles have been honed and made better and applied. The Software Engineering Institute at Carnegie Mellon University has done a lot of work, and it introduced the concept of the Capability Maturity Model. Herein processes were defined which can be applied to software development projects so that defects can be prevented from entering the software system being developed. Then there were some statistical techniques developed which helped to predict and measure the number of defects in the software system. A pioneering work was done at Motorola in the 1980s which was later known as Six Sigma. In this process, which is based on complexity and size, the technology and process utilized in software development are analyzed and the number of defects is predicted at each stage in software development (conception, design, and build). Once the number of defects is known, they are identified using software testing techniques and removed.

Traditionally, once software is built, it is handed over to the software testing team to test it and find defects. The team uses many techniques including exploratory testing, functional testing, regression testing, performance testing, stress testing, and so on, to find as many defects as possible. These defects are then fixed by the development team and then the testing team retests them. Once they are fixed, the software is retested again. This cycle continues as per test plan as to how many iterations of testing are to be performed. If the number of iterations of testing reaches the number of cycles as per test plans, then even if some defects are not fixed, the software is handed over for deployment with a list of known defects. Apart from the defects found by the test team, the application is bound to have defects that will be detected by end users during the use of the application. These again have to be fixed or a work-around has to be provided, but this time around the cost of fixing them will be too high.

1.13   Software Testing Methodologies

Software engineering standards like Capability Maturity Model, ISO9000, and so on, addressed many process-related problems in software development and helped in evolving a matured Software Development Life Cycle (SDLC). But they failed in evolving processes for software testing. For instance, in SDLC there is one phase for software testing. In this model it is assumed that software requirements, software design, and software build phases have no role in software testing. But, in fact, this is not true. From best practices derived from executing software projects over the years, it has been proved that software testing processes should be involved right from the software requirements phase itself. So a software test model has evolved to address these issues. It is known as the Test Maturity Model (TMM). This model states a process known as Software Test Life Cycle (STLC). Most of the processes associated with STLC—such as requirement review, design review, test coverage, test planning, test strategy, resource allocation, test automation, test case preparation, test execution, test reporting, defect tracking, risk management, version control, test bed preparation, software configuration, and so on—are spread over all the phases of SDLC and a parallel STLC process exists for any of the SDLC processes.

1.14   Tools

There are tools on the market for many tasks associated with software testing. There are tools available for test management, test case generation, test automation, defect tracking, and so on. Some of the areas where tools do not work include test case generation and test planning. Test case generation is not a task that can be automated easily because a lot of thinking is required in writing test cases which is not possible to automate easily. Similarly test planning requires a lot of thinking on things like technology, effort, resource availability, skills availability, infrastructure availability, and so on.

1.14.1   Test Case Execution Automation

Test case execution has gained the most from the introduction of automation tools. There are some great tools out there in the market which can do good automation for functional testing, performance testing, load testing, regression testing, smoke testing, and so on. The biggest player in this market is Mercury Interactive (now part of Hewlett Packard) with Quick Test Pro, Load Runner, and Win Runner tools. Some other vendors include Selenium from ThoughtWorks and Certify from Worksoft.

1.14.2 Test Coverage

Test coverage tools enable the test team to know how much of the software application will be covered under the present test project. Test coverage analysis is done either using code insertion techniques in the source code of the software application or using external code to check which components of the software application under test will be covered for testing. Rational PureCoverage from IBM, TCAT from Software Research Inc., and McCabe IQ from McCabe Software are some tools that do test coverage analysis.

1.14.3 Defect Tracking

Defect tracking tools allow reporting of defects and tracking of defect life cycle in a team environment. Test Track Pro from Seapine Software, BugZilla from Mozilla, and ClearQuest from IBM are such tools in this category.

1.14.4 Test Management

Test management involves the design and creation of test cases, test case execution, keeping and updating inventory of test cases, and so on. Test management also involves keeping and updating inventory of automation scripts. Versions of test cases and automation scripts are also managed here. Some of the tools available in the market include Test Director from Mercury Interactive (now part of Hewlett Packard), Silk Plan Pro from Segue Software, and QA Director from Compuware.

1.15   Project Offshoring

No discussion on software development can be considered complete without a mention of software project offshoring. Offshoring has brought a new dimension to software development. There has been a radical shift in many aspects of software development. In their eagerness to compete and get more business, companies have ensured that distance, culture, and time zone constraints do not interfere in providing unmatched productivity, quality, and costs to their customers. Software project offshoring service providers have armed themselves with mature software engineering processes. Robust processes have been followed, ensuring a substantial reduction in software defects.

1.16   Testing Being Commoditized?

Coupled with the benefits of offshoring, now it is possible to commoditize software testing. For this, offshoring service providers have started the practice of setting up a centralized testing organization. Whenever any project comes, it is put into a queue. The organization evaluates for resource requirements and then allocates it to the project. The project starts when the allocated resources become available for the project. The project is executed and when finished, it is delivered to the customer. This kind of organization structure requires special processing departments and processing line similar to matrix manufacturing organization structures where we have production lines and processing departments.

There is a paradigm shift here. You no longer have discrete projects as in the traditional approach. Resources in the traditional project execution approach were tied to specific projects and were not shared across projects. But in this case we have special processing zones popularly called "Centers of Excellence" (CoE for short) from where each project buys some time and resources are shared among all projects that need this special processing. For instance, we can have CoE for automating functional test cases using Mercury Interactive's Quick Text Pro (QTP) tool. Automation engineers belonging to this CoE write the automation script for the project where automation script written in QTP is required and deliver it to the concerned project. Business analysts belonging to another CoE (which specializes in creating test cases for the financial domain) get requirements and design of the project and write functional test cases and deliver it to the concerned project.

This way of doing things increases productivity tremendously. This results in substantially lower costs, and the project schedule also shrinks. Quality is ensured by requiring fanatical adherence to software engineering process models.

1.17   Conclusion

Software testing is so important that any software vendor or internal software development team cannot overlook it.

Sometime back I was working as a subject matter expert for a software vendor who was developing a product that will do production planning, material planning, and distribution planning for manufacturing and distribution companies. They bagged some orders from customers while the product was still under development. The development team worked round the clock to finish the product and deliver it to customers. The development team consisted of some bright guys, and they delivered the projects within the scheduled time. Everything looked fine at this moment. Customers were happy that the product was delivered in time, and the development team was rejoicing. But within a month, everything changed. The company was flooded with reports of thousands of severe defects from each of the customers. For the next 9 months the company received tens of thousands of reports of severe defects from customers. Within 2 years the company was forced to close down as customers brought lawsuits that the company found difficult to battle. What was the reason for this kind of fate for this software vendor? Lack of software testing! In fact, this company did not have any budget for testing at all. So no testers were employed and no testing team was in place. Developers tested their own code and that was it. Not testing its product caused the company to pay a heavy price.

This was an extreme case. But even in normal circumstances, the importance of software testing cannot be ignored. Software testing costs money, but not doing software testing costs more!

Chapter 2

Kinds of Software Testing Projects

After going through Chapter 1, you may have understood some basic concepts in software development, software testing, and software testing management.

So far so good!

Coming to software testing types, you may need to understand concepts of what needs to be tested, why it should be tested, and how it will be tested.

2.1 Software Testing Types

There are different kinds of software applications out there to be used for fulfilling different needs of the users. There are enterprise resource planning (ERP) and big enterprise software applications that are used by global corporations to do their everyday business on the one hand, and there are desktop applications to be used by individual persons for fulfilling a variety of needs like word processing, calculations, entertainment, training, and so on, on the other hand. Then there are different platforms on which the software application runs. Again software applications have different architectures. The software application development process also differs from one place to another. To take care of these variations, there are many types of software testing.

Let us have a look at some of the software testing types:

- **Black box testing**—The majority of software testing can be classified as black box testing. Here the tester need not know software design or code. These tests are based on requirements and functionality.

■ **White box testing**—White box testing is mostly done by developers. It is based on knowledge of the internal logic of an application's code. Tests are based on coverage of code statements, branches, paths, conditions, loops, and so on. For white box testing, test coverage is also done so that how much of the application has been tested in a release is known.

■ **Unit testing**—Unit testing is done by developers themselves. It is the most "micro" scale of testing, to test particular functions or code modules. It is typically done by the programmer and not by testers, as it requires detailed knowledge of the internal program design and code. It is not always easily done unless the application has a well-designed architecture with tight code; it may require developing test driver modules or test harnesses.

■ **Incremental integration testing**—Continuous testing of an application as new functionality is added requires that various aspects of an application's functionality be independent enough to work separately before all parts of the program are completed or that test drivers be developed as needed; it is done by programmers or by testers.

■ **Integration testing**—Testing of combined parts of an application to determine if they function together correctly. The parts can be code modules, individual applications, client and server applications on a network, and so on. This type of testing is especially relevant to client/server and distributed systems.

■ **Functional testing**—Black box–type testing geared to functional requirements of an application; this type of testing should be done by testers. This does not mean that the programmers should not check that their code works before releasing it (which of course applies to any stage of testing).

■ **System testing**—Black box–type testing that is based on overall requirements specifications; it covers all combined parts of a system. In the hierarchy of testing types, system testing comes below user acceptance testing. It does not cover integration testing, which is done to ensure that the software product works well with other software products with which it has to be integrated.

■ **End-to-end testing**—Similar to system testing, end-to-end testing represents the "macro" end of the test scale; it involves testing of a complete application environment in a situation that mimics real-world use, such as interacting with a database, using network communications, or interacting with other hardware, applications, or systems if appropriate.

■ **Sanity testing or smoke testing**—Typically an initial testing effort to determine if a new software version is performing well enough to accept it for a major testing effort. For example, if the new software is crashing systems every 5 minutes, bogging down systems to a crawl, or corrupting databases, the software may not be in a "sane" enough condition to warrant further testing in its current state.

■ **Regression testing**—Retesting after fixes or modifications of the software or its environment. It can be difficult to determine how much retesting is needed, especially near the end of the development cycle. Automated testing tools can be especially useful for this type of testing.

- **Acceptance testing**—Final testing based on specifications of the end user or customer or based on use by end users/customers over some limited period of time.

- **Load testing**—Testing an application under heavy loads, such as testing of a Web site under a range of loads to determine at what point the system's response time degrades or fails. Also known as performance testing.

- **Stress testing**—Term often used interchangeably with *load testing* and *performance testing*. Also used to describe such tests as system functional testing while under unusually heavy loads, heavy repetition of certain actions or inputs, input of large numerical values, large complex queries to a database system, and so on.

- **Performance testing**—Term often used interchangeably with *stress testing* and *load testing*. Ideally performance testing (or any other type of testing) is defined in requirements documentation or QA or test plans.

- **Usability testing**—Testing for user-friendliness. Clearly this is subjective and will depend on the targeted end user or customer. User interviews, surveys, video recording of user sessions, and other techniques can be used. Programmers and testers are usually not appropriate as usability testers.

- **Install/uninstall testing**—Testing of full, partial, or upgrade install/uninstall processes.

- **Recovery testing**—Testing how well a system recovers from crashes, hardware failures, or other catastrophic problems.

- **Failover testing**—Typically used interchangeably with *recovery testing*.

- **Security testing**—Testing how well the system protects against unauthorized internal or external access, willful damage, and so on; it may require sophisticated testing techniques.

- **Compatibility testing**—Testing how well software performs within the environment of a particular hardware, software, operating system, network, and so on.

- **Exploratory testing**—Often taken to mean a creative, informal software test that is not based on formal test plans or test cases. In exploratory testing, testers may be learning the software as they test it. But more importantly exploratory testing is the place where most of the defects in the software are caught. The reason is that even if you create comprehensive test cases to cover most of the software application for testing, it is not enough. Exploratory testing testers use their experience and knowledge of the application to test the application thoroughly, which is not possible using any structured approach to testing such as using test cases to test the software application.

- **Ad hoc testing**—Same as exploratory testing with a difference that ad hoc testing is used more in cases where no formal test planning is used.

- **Context-driven testing**—Testing driven by an understanding of the environment, culture, and intended use of software. Context is very important because it determines things like criticality, minute functionality, accepted level of software application failure, and so on. An application that is meant to be used by people for getting online information through a portal will be very different from a software application that is being used for taking care of accounting functions for any company. Similarly software to be used for any country's defense department program should be very secure, and the threat of its being used by an unauthorized person should be completely taken care of. So the cases mentioned above require that the software be tested thoroughly for performance, transaction integrity, and security respectively.

■ **User acceptance testing**—This is one of the most common kinds of testing, and almost all software projects have user acceptance testing (UAT). UAT provides a report that helps in determining if the software is satisfactory to an end user or customer. UAT is done based on the user requirements that were documented and based on which the software was developed.

■ **Comparison testing**—Comparing software weaknesses and strengths to competing products. This is essentially used for marketing purposes to highlight the strengths of one's own software application compared to that of competitors. Some third-party software evaluation and software selection service providers also use comparison testing to provide unbiased reports about competing software products.

■ **Alpha testing**—Testing of an application when development is nearing completion; minor design changes may still be made as a result of such testing. Typically alpha testing is done by end users or others, not by programmers or testers. After alpha testing the software, the defects found in alpha testing can be fixed and the application can be released for beta testing.

■ **Beta testing**—Testing when development and testing by an internal team are completed and final defects and problems need to be found before final release. Typically beta testing is done by end users or others and not by programmers or testers. Beta testing is important because the defects reported by beta testers can still be fixed before the application is released to final end customers.

■ **Mutation testing**—A method for determining if a set of test data or test cases is useful, by deliberately introducing various code changes (defects) and retesting with the original test data/cases to determine if the defects are detected. Proper implementation requires large computational resources. Mutation testing is also used in conjunction with test coverage analysis by introducing defects at different parts of the application to know whether that part of the application has to be tested.

■ **Agile testing**—Agile testing is done in conjunction with projects on which agile or extreme programming methodologies are used. They involve similar approaches to those followed in agile or extreme programming methodologies.

■ **Back-to-back testing**—A kind of functional testing where two or more similar components of the application under test are given the same input and results are compared.

- **Benchmark test**—When any component or the complete application is tested with a view to compare it against a similar component or application. The benchmark test is used mainly for marketing purposes to compare any application with an application that is considered as an industry leader.
- **Big bang testing**—When a software application is integrated with another application, a lot of integration testing will be required to be performed. This can be done in phases. But sometimes it can be taken in one go. Big bang testing is the method to test complete integration under one phase.
- **Business process-based testing**—Nowadays most enterprise-level software applications (in the category of ERP, CRM, SCM, etc., applications) have rich functionality that also contains complete business process functions. Subject matter experts (SME) test these functions to ensure that all the steps in business transaction and workflows work as per specifications. The SME does not follow the menu hierarchy and instead follows the business flow to test the complete business transactions. This kind of testing is known as business process-based testing.

2.2 What Needs to Be Tested?

Software is developed for many uses. In fact, in today's world, we cannot visualize our lives without the presence of software around us. It is everywhere. Software is used for doing financial management, financial calculations, financial reporting, trade management, order management, customer management, operations management (also known as supply chain management), logistics management, spend management, retail management, supplier management, hospital management, etc. These are examples of enterprise management software. Then there are desktop applications that need to be tested (e.g. Microsoft Word, Microsoft Project, Microsoft Visio, Notepad). There are software applications that act as interfaces with the hardware part of computers. These are called device drivers. There are software systems for operating mobiles, cars, airplanes, industrial and safety equipment, and so on. These are called embedded systems. There are communication applications for the telecom sector as well as instant messengers and VOIP systems, which use networking protocols, ports, and many peripheral telecom devices to operate. And who can forget e-mail programs, without which so much of our communication needs would not be fulfilled.

Most of these software systems are used for commercial purposes (more than 90% of all software development is done for commercial purposes). Software is also used for military, scientific research, and space missions.

Software development can also be classified as product development, application development, custom software development, and customization. Testing of these systems is also different. When a software product is being developed, it involves creating a broad and rich functionality so that the software can be used by many customers; sometimes even millions of customers use it. Examples of such software include ERP systems from big software vendors like SAP AG, Oracle, Microsoft, Siebel, Click Commerce, SSG Global, and so on. These software products are called packaged software applications. If installation of the packaged software application requires not much effort by the user and he installs it himself using only some clicks of his computer mouse, then that software is called a shrink-wrapped software application. Many times, these ERPs do not fit into the requirement of any company and in those cases, the company decides to develop a software application from scratch which caters to the specific needs of that company. Software applications thus developed are called custom software. Then there are cases when the packaged application can be customized to fit the requirements of the company. In such cases this process is known as customization of the software application.

In this book, software testing management for software products and applications is covered along with testing requirements for custom software. Even when custom software applications are not specifically written, the context will apply to them as well.

So basically we can divide types of software products into enterprise systems, desktop systems, device drivers, communication programs, and embedded systems. Testing approaches for these categories will be very different from each other. Desktop, device driver, and embedded system types mainly involve client system testing, whereas enterprise systems may involve both client and server testing. Types of systems can be mainframe, client-server, or browser-server based (Internet or intranet system where client is the browser). With the advent of thin clients and Internet technologies, nowadays enterprise systems involve almost always only server testing. The client part is only a browser. Then again, these enterprise systems involve multitier architecture. The database is a separate logical tier, and most of the time it is a separate physical tier; furthermore, the database is installed on a dedicated separate box (computer) or more than one box. The server can be divided into a Web server and an application server. Each of these servers can be installed on a dedicated box or more than one box. The architectures of software applications have been changing over time. Currently most of the applications are Web based where the client is only a browser and client installations are not required. All the software is installed on the server.

2.3   Enterprise System Testing

Enterprise systems are characterized by large size, many concurrent users, and many kinds of users using different functionalities of the application. Enterprise systems need to be tested for functional as well as nonfunctional testing. You need to test the system from what is mentioned in the requirements as well as how it has been designed. The nonfunctional aspects include whether the system is scalable, whether the system can take the stress of heavy user load, whether the system can withstand a sudden surge of load at peak times, and so on. One must also take into account the fact that some part of the system is behind the firewall (e.g., intranet) and some part of the system is outside the firewall. Because most of the systems nowadays are at least partly over the Internet, security issues are paramount. Elaborate security mechanisms should be provided in the system to prevent hacking, unauthorized access, phishing (a process of impersonating an authentic user and stealing financial information about somebody from a Web site using stolen personal information), and so on.

Most organizations have legacy as well as new systems implemented. Similarly the organizations may have many systems implemented at their premises. All these heterogeneous systems should be properly integrated, and so one aspect of enterprise application testing is testing whether integration with other applications is working properly.

So you, as a testing professional, need to test for many aspects of the application like integration, security, functionality, and performance.

Functionality of the system for different versions is different. So you also need to do regression testing to ensure that the new components added in new versions have not affected functionality of existing components and that component features work as defined in the requirement document. Similarly, in the same components, if new features have been added, then check to ensure that old features are working as expected.

Once the system is fully developed, it has to be tested in its entirety. For this, pre-UAT (pre-user acceptance testing, also called system testing) and finally UAT testing have to be done.

In essence, enterprise systems are large and complex and have a large functionality. Testing of these systems requires prior experience and knowledge.

2.4 Enterprise System Types

2.4.1 Banking, Finance, Insurance, and Securities (BFSI) Systems

Out of all enterprise systems, BFSI systems are the most prevalent and widely used. By their very nature, software systems are the most useful tools for BFSI companies. BFSI systems crucially depend on calculation, creation, and collection of data from many sources. They are transaction intensive and need security to ensure that transaction data is not going to any unauthorized source.

BFSI enterprise systems need to be tested for transaction integrity, secure access, and integration capability for integration with other systems.

2.4.2 Enterprise Resource Planning (ERP) Systems

ERP systems are the biggest software applications, comprising many subapplications for areas covering finance, supply chain management (SCM), manufacturing, customer relationship management (CRM), project management, supplier management, and so on. Different modules have their specific requirements for testing. For instance, CRM applications work on intelligence and a big part consists of data mining and data conversion.

Software testing in this case will involve testing data integrity during data mining and data consistency during data conversion. Similarly other modules need specialized testing along with the usual testing that is required for enterprise systems.

2.5 Desktop System Testing

Any application that is installed on a client machine and is used by the users of that application for tasks such as calculations, letter preparation, project plan preparation, drawings, operating system, and so on, is called a desktop application. These systems have no server components and do not need computer networks for their work.

For testing these kinds of systems, you may not need to bother about databases, servers, and networks. You also do not need to bother about integration, as these systems are stand-alone applications. But these applications have a lot of features that are invoked through menus, function keys, toolbar buttons, and different forms available from inside the application itself. At installation some features can be configured. Many other features can be configured through options available from inside the application itself.

Some amount of white box testing is involved here to change/modify/remove features to test the system thoroughly. Then regression, pre-UAT, UAT, and any other suitable form of testing may be performed.

2.6 Device Driver System Testing

Device drivers are the interface between computer hardware, human user, and computer operating system. Some of them include graphic, sound, keyboard, mouse, digital cameras, and networking cards. Once a device driver is installed for a specific device on a computer operating system, that device can be attached to that computer and will work.

Device drivers are basically stand-alone desktop applications and do not integrate with other applications. They are implemented as services on the operating system. Many of these drivers are resource-intensive programs and require a lot of computer memory and processing power of the CPU to operate (e.g., some high-power graphic and sound drivers).

Testing of these applications requires a good knowledge of the operating system, device functionality, memory, and processing power usage of the computer system. So these device drivers are tested against their intended functionality, performance related to memory and processing power usage, and integration with the operating system.

2.7 Stage of Software Life Cycle

Most people are familiar with software testing activities that are done in regular software development projects. In most books and literature, these activities have been covered in detail. But few books have covered testing activities performed in the production environment. Internet applications need to be tested regularly when they are in production. They have become mission-critical applications for the companies who run them. Similarly enterprise applications that are Web based, which many users from customers and suppliers along with company employees use to do their work, also need to be tested periodically to ensure that users are able to use the applications and that there is no downtime due to any hardware or software problems. This is more critical for hosted applications, as the company who owns the hosted application earns its revenue from subscriptions. They charge their users by the number of transactions performed in a week or month. Downtime is a complete no-no for these hosted application vendors. So they periodically check functionality and availability of their application to users.

2.8 Outsourced Software Testing

An independent software verification and validation service is a new trend that has gained momentum over the last 10 years. Here any software application is to be tested by a software testing service provider. It has been felt that using outsourcing and offshoring coupled with consolidation of projects can bring about tremendous benefits to customers. With mature models, software testing has become an independent component in the software development which can be outsourced separately from software development. Many software service providers have come up with business models that drive a lot of business value to their customers.

Due to scattered team structures, vast distance between customer and service provider locations, different cultures, and many other factors, the delivery model has changed significantly for these projects. A detailed discussion is provided in Chapter 11 of this book.

2.8.1 Software Vendor Perspective

If you happen to be working for a software vendor, then you will either be testing products of your own company or be managing service providers who are testing products on your company's behalf. If you happen to be in the second situation, then you will have to manage a lot of other things than technology and people. Now you have deal with different cultures, complying with different governmental regulations, time differences due to people located in different time zones, different productivity, and many more hurdles.

Software testing projects are no different, and you should learn about these things and try to concentrate on these issues more than the technical aspects of your project.

2.8.2 Software Service Provider Perspective

The drivers for software services are low cost, better quality, and have a mature delivery model. Test managers from service providers are always eager to provide these values to their customers.

When it comes to delivering goods, the test manager banks heavily on the delivery model. He will have to make sure that the transition of the project happens smoothly. He will have to resort to a safe transition using techniques like going for a pilot project and knowledge transfer to his team from the existing team that was working on that project. He will have to make a plan to train his offshore staff to make them understand what customer expectations are and what kind of quality is expected on their assignments. He will have to make sure that the delivery model is foolproof and that there will not be any hiccups down the road.

The test manager's role is double-edged. He has to be strong technically to deliver the goods and have the will have to take care of bottlenecks involved in offshoring the project.

2.9 Performance Testing

Most of the testing areas and types of testing are basically related to functional and usability testing. But with the advent of Internet, things have changed. There are Web sites that carry the latest business, technology, social, and current affairs news and information. Some other Web sites act as social networking portals where people meet and exchange ideas through multimedia, documents, and other kinds of information. There are other sites that act as business exchange portals. Then there are sites that allow people to create and host blogs on their sites. Then there are sites that provide free e-mail service to their users. Some other users access these sites to search the Internet for information.

These kinds of sites are accessed by millions of users from all around the world. At any point in time millions of users will be accessing the site simultaneously. Due to the huge load on these sites created by millions of users accessing the site concurrently, performance issues arise. Many users may not be able to access the site within an acceptable time limit due to excessive load on the servers. Many users may not get access to the site at all due to the same reasons. Some other users may experience performance issues in accessing some particular pages of the Web site.

The profitability of these sites depends on the traffic (number of users accessing the sites) the sites generate. They provide most of the content and services on their sites free of cost to their users. They get their revenue from advertising. An increase in the number of users means an increase in advertising revenue. So, from a business perspective, it is essential that the performance of their sites be good even when the load on their servers is huge. Generally, if any page requires more than 10 seconds to load, then the performance of the application is considered poor.

To make sure that their site performance is good, they need to test their site for performance. Performance bottlenecks could be at user interface, database, server memory, server processor speed, or any networking component at the Web server farm consisting of server computers, application interfaces, network routers, and so on.

Let us look at some of the issues involved in performance testing:

- **User interface**—If the software developers have used big-file-sized images or any user interface components, then they take time to load in the page. This results in poor performance. If poor performance is encountered, then the developers should replace these heavy components with light components to improve performance.
- **Database queries**—If the software developers have used queries that take a long time to fetch data and show results, then this results in poor performance. The software developers should have a good knowledge of what kind of query is being fired for any user action and how to tune database queries for optimal performance. If database queries are the bottlenecks for poor application performance, then they should be tuned further to improve performance.

2.10   Security Testing

With advancements in technology, hackers and data thieves also have access to tools to intrude into secure sites and steal personal and financial data. They use phishing, personification, Trojan horses, and viruses to attack users' personal computers or servers and steal data.

As Internet use continues to increase, these threats will keep increasing in the future. Companies and users alike will keep taking advantage of the Internet. A user can access his bank account and do transactions using his home computer. He does not have to go to the bank branch to do these transactions. Similarly the bank will have to provide less service at the branch as the number of customers visiting the branch declines substantially. This saves a lot of money for the bank. So the Internet provides benefits to both the bank and its customers.

Portals and Internet sites must provide thorough checks to ensure that these thefts do not happen. These applications must be tested thoroughly to ensure that safety mechanisms provided in these applications work properly. For these reasons security testing is increasing day by day.

In security testing, at one end features and functions are tested so that they are available only to the roles as intended in the design of the application. At the other end, each application is tested to ensure that unauthorized access is denied by the application. During transactions, it is ensured that the data being transmitted either from the user or from the server is encrypted and cannot be decrypted. So a credit card number sent by a user is encrypted immediately and is received by the server in encrypted form. A decryption software will then decrypt this data.

Chapter 3

Software Testing Project Strategies

In Indian folk songs (Asian, not North American!), they sing prayers about drinks and the beauty of women. But the words have deeper meanings. In fact, they are speaking about spirituality and the divinity of God and not about earthly things. Similarly documents about your project may have deeper meanings. So you need to scratch the surface and find out the real issues they are talking about.

Many times the users themselves are not sure what they want. So the requirements you get from these types of users are never accurate or complete. Accordingly the design and coding will have many iterations. In each iteration, the features are refined and accordingly the design is changed.

Any project will be doomed to fail if suitable strategies for executing that project are not well planned and well implemented.

Strategies will include how best to utilize your resources and time available to you against risk factors to achieve the best results for your project in terms of agreed-upon deliverables, customer perception, fulfilling company objectives, and so on.

In this chapter we will discuss making strategies for automation, resource utilization, technology management, risk management, and so on.

To create good strategies for test projects, let us first understand the life cycle of a software product and how to best align software testing with different phases of the product life cycle. Later we can learn how automation is linked in the life cycle.

3.1 Strategy versus Planning

Before we think about making planning for our project, we must first come up with some strategy to deal with risks, probable tasks involved, technology selection, skills matching, required training, automation, tools, automation framework, and so on. Planning is restricted more or less to making schedules, allocating resources, selecting tools, deciding on the number of tests to be created and executed, deciding on defect life cycle, and so on. Accordingly, test management should have a hierarchy of test strategy, test planning, test execution, and analysis and reporting.

3.2 Complexity Management

Life was very simple before the old dark days, when the monster mainframe computers had not yet been introduced, sometime just after the Stone Age. No computers, no modern-day gizmos, no worries about project deadlines, no worries about facing a dominating boss, no worries about not being able to complete assigned tasks in time. In short, life was beautiful. But life started becoming less beautiful once computers started coming round the corner. Life started becoming a little more complicated. People started worrying about customer expectations, customer requirements, software design, software architecture, software builds, software versions, going live, production environments, defect fixes, code reviews, code walkthroughs, and of course software testing.

With computing power doubling every 2 years over the last 50 years or so, bigger and more powerful software applications have been developed and deployed. It is said that resources at hand are limited, but the human appetite for more has also fueled the monstrous growth of software systems. At some time human beings were more than happy with a computing speed of 28 kHz. Now any ordinary computer comes with 3014 MHz.

More and more of the work is being taken away from human beings and being assigned to computers. Increases in computing power and in the ability to gather and enter business data from any geographic site into a central computer database are helping companies to grow and establish themselves in many geographic regions of the world and thus become truly global enterprises. And they are expanding quickly too, thanks to these ubiquitous computers. Without computers, such behemoth enterprises are unthinkable.

With such growth in the size of software systems, the complexity of software systems has also grown.

With the increasing size and complexity of software systems, their testing has also become more and more complex. You, as a software professional, have to accept this fact and make improvements in your own skill sets to deal with it. Not only the size and complexity but also the architecture, programming languages used, and so on, are also changing with the increasing pace.

To test modern-day software systems, you need to master the latest testing techniques and methodologies to combat the systems' large size and complexity and become successful in testing these systems.

For the test manager, to deal with testing any such huge and complex system is the old and proven divide-and-rule methodology. Have a mug of beer (if you are a teetotaler, then maybe you can do the Mountain Dew) and sit down with a paper and pencil. Do not panic yet (keep it for later)! If you have previous experience with managing a similar test project (even if it was a smaller monster compared to the present one) and if you remember the details, then you are almost there. If not, then you can search your company archives to find out if any similar project was ever executed and if any project data is available. If you fail here, then there is still one more avenue available for your rescue. Your friends! If your friends fail, then you have the ultimate tool at your disposal: Google and the Internet! Find it there through searches, forums, and so on. If that fails, then read this book. So you are there! Now you can easily manage the show. Have lots of confidence and be positive!

If you also possess domain knowledge (e.g., supply chain management, finance, telecom) and the project belongs to your domain, then you are in a safe boat. If domain is not your cup of tea, then do not worry! There is still some hope out there. You can take help from your same old and trusted friends, Google and the Internet.

You have come to the conclusion that the project is big and complex because you have heard about it from the delivery and senior managers. But if you remember correctly, then you must have seen the requirements and design documents. They are the lifeline for you. Without them, you cannot survive. So take good care of them and go through them again and again. After you go through them four times, you will see light at the end of the dark tunnel. You will have a good picture of what is required for the project. You will also have a good idea of what is to be done and how to do it.

Humor apart, you can win over complexity by the same old divide-and-rule methodology. Actually complexity comes either from big size or from the intricacy of things. If something is intricate, you can enlarge its image and then you can have a big picture with less intricacy. So you cut pieces from the enlarged image and now you can see simpler things. If the size is already big, then you can cut pieces to make them manageable.

In the case of software testing projects, complexity plays its role mostly in functional testing. The best approach is that you divide the software application into modules and then divide the modules into submodules. Once it is done, you can then understand functionality, workflows, and all other aspects for each of these components. Once you understand each and every piece, summing them up gives you the bigger picture.

The following case study is a good example of dealing with complexity.

3.2.1 Case Study on Complexity Management

Once I worked as a domain expert on a test project. There was one module that was very difficult to test.

3.2.1.1   Module Description

This module was used for making automatic appointments of trucks at dock doors of warehouses based on various constraints, availability, and priority. The constraints were of two types—hard and soft constraints—and there was a clear hierarchy as to which constraint would apply first and which would apply after the other constraint. At the same time, hard constraints can never be overridden but the soft constraint can be overridden if certain conditions are met. Overall the logic for this program was very complex, so testing this logic was difficult.

3.2.1.2   Strategy

It was recognized very early in the project that testing of this module was very difficult and special attention was needed to test it. A series of brainstorming sessions was organized until complete understanding of the logic was acquired and an appropriate test strategy was developed. It took five such sessions of 1 hour each. Because appointments were affected by existing appointments, it was decided to test the engine with transaction data present in the system. Whenever the engine did not return with the most suitable appointment, it was verified in the calendar whether this suitable appointment slot was already occupied by an existing appointment. Then multiple shipments originating from different pickup locations were combined. Combined shipments were also to be tested.

3.2.1.3   Complexity

There were 11 main constraints. Some of the constraints had up to 20 subconstraints. Existing transaction data also came into play because when any existing appointment was present, the engine would have to find another appointment slot. The output of the module was to provide appointment start and end time for any incoming truck at any appropriate dock door (as suggested by the appointment engine) of the warehouse. The inputs were pickup warehouse, delivery warehouse, truck capacity, truck type, kind of goods loaded on the truck, truck start time after pickup, truck arrival time at the delivery warehouse, kind of goods that can be received at a particular dock door, number of dock doors at a specific warehouse, opening and closing time of dock doors on different days of the week, calendar or business week defined in the calendar for the dock door, partner preference for loading or unloading at dock doors, availability of QA (quality assurance) at dock doors, availability of labor for loading or unloading, time window under which any shipment must be appointed at any dock door, maximum number of shipments from a particular partner or type of load that can be received at a dock door, size restriction at dock doors for specific maximum loads at certain times during a day, preferred start times, and so on.

After evaluating the constraints, current time, shipment time, existing appointments, and calendars, the engine would come up with three suggested appointments and display the data on the screen. The user then could choose any of these appointments, or if he did not like any of the options, then he could try to create a manual appointment by entering it on the screen. If the user tried to make a manual appointment, then the engine would again run to see if any existing appointment conflicted with this appointment. If there were no conflicts, then this appointment could be saved. If not, then the user could again input appointment start and end times and try.

3.2.1.4 Problems

When the test cycle was going to start, nobody in the test team had any idea how to test this module or how complex the module was. It was a real challenge to test it. Even in the SRS (software requirement specification) and SDD (system design document) documents the complete logic was not stated anywhere. It was provided in fragments.

3.2.1.5 Solution

To test this module, I had to write the complete logic. Basically two calculations had to be done: (1) calculate variable load times and (2) calculate start and end times of appointment. Calculation of variable load times was easy. But calculation of appointment start and end times was difficult. One strategy to test was to keep all constraints constant, get one shipment record, and deduce the appointment start and end times from reading, passing, and comparing one constraint to the other in their hierarchy until you reach the end. The final output will be the appointment times. Write down your result, and then run the engine and find what the engine suggested and compare it with your result. If the engine produced the right result, then the test case will pass. Then change the value of one constraint, keeping values for other constraints the same as previous values, and then run the engine again for the same shipment data. Do this for each constraint with separate test cases. Overall we needed some 500 test cases to test the engine thoroughly.

3.2.1.6 Pseudo Logic

I am providing here the pseudo logic that I had made to test the module.

3.2.1.6.1 Load Time Settings Decision Logic

```
If partner Variation is true then
        If variable load time then
                If calculated load time > Max reservation time
then
                        load time = max reservation time
                    elseif calculated load time < Min reservation
```

```
time then
                    load time = min reservation time
            else load time = calculated load time
        else load time = fixed load time
end if
elseIf default receiving load time is true then

        if default receiving load time = fixed load time then

                load time = fixed default receiving load time
        elseif default receiving load time = variable load
time then
                If calculated load time > Max reservation time
then
                    load time = max reservation time
            elseif calculated load time < Min reservation
time then
                    load time = min reservation time
            else load time = calculated load time
            end if
        end if
else load time = default reservation time
endif
note: calculated load time = higher (of shipped qty. 1 or
shipped qty 2) * loading rate + load time per distinct item *
item count
```

3.2.1.6.2   Complete Appointment Scheduling Logic

```
If [(shipment date) < Today's Date] then
        Message "Shipment is out dated and no appointment can
be done"
else
Appointment date = (shipment date + pre date tolerance(i)) or
(shipment date - pre date tolerance(i))
If Frequency count on shipment date < Max Frequency Limit]
for partner, partner profile name, load type or appointment
code then
If Shipment Time >= Now + Reservation Lead Time
and (Now + Reservation Lead Time) Not Between Size
Restriction then
                        Appointment date = (shipment date
- pre date tolerance(i)) Date
                        If Round(Now + Reservation Lead
Time) Start Time Slots = Preferred Start Time then

If Round(Previous Appointment End Time) Start Time Slot =<
Preferred Start Time then
```

```
If Round(Next Appointment Start Time) Start Time Slot >=
Preferred Start Time then
If Preferred Start Time + Load Time =< Next Appointment Start
Time then
If Preferred Start Time within Work shift / Work Hour range then
Appointment Start Time = Preferred Start Time
                                    End if
ElseIf Round(Previous Appointment End Time) Start Time Slot +
Load Time =< Next Appointment Time then
Appointment Start Time = Round(Previous Appointment End Time)
                                              EndIf
                                    EndIf
                          EndIf
                Else
If Round(Now + Reservation Lead Time) Start Time Slots >=
Previous Appointment End Time then
If Round(Previous Appointment End Time) Start Time Slot + Load
Time =< Next Appointment Start Time then
Appointment Start Time = Round(Now + Reservation Lead Time)
Start Time Slots
                                        EndIf
                              EndIf
                    Endif
              Endif
          Else go to Shipment Date + post date tolerance(i))


                    If Frequency on (shipment date + post date
tolerance(i)) count < Max Frequency Limit for partner, partner
profile name, load type or appointment code then

If Shipment Time >= Now + Reservation Lead Time and (Now +
Reservation Lead Time) Not Between Size Restriction then

                              Appointment date = (Shipment
Date + 1)
                              If Round(Now + Reservation
Lead Time) Start Time Slots = Preferred Start Time then
If Round(Previous Appointment End Time) Start Time Slot =<
Preferred Start Time then
If Round(Next Appointment Start Time) Start Time Slot >=
Preferred Start Time then
If Preferred Start Time + Load Time =< Next Appointment Start
Time then
Appointment Start Time = Preferred Start Time
ElseIf Round(Previous Appointment End Time) Start Time Slot +
Load Time =< Next Appointment Time then
Appointment Start Time = Round(Previous Appointment End Time)
```

```
                                                        EndIf
                                              EndIf
                                    EndIf
                          Else
If Round(Now + Reservation Lead Time) Start Time Slots >=
Previous Appointment End Time then
If Round(Previous Appointment End Time) Start Time Slot + Load
Time =< Next Appointment Start Time then
Appointment Start Time = Round(Now + Reservation Lead Time)
Start Time Slots
                                              EndIf
                                    EndIf
                          Endif
                    Endif
                    Exit if appointment found
post date tolerance(i) = post date tolerance(i+1)
Else go to (Shipment Date – pre date tolerance(i)) where
(shipment date – pre date tolerance(i)) >= Today's Date

If Frequency on [(shipment date - 1) count < Max Frequency
Limit] and [(shipment date - 1) > Today's Date] for partner,
partner profile name, load type or appointment code then

If Shipment Time >= Now + Reservation Lead Time and (Now +
Reservation Lead Time) Not Between Size Restriction then

                              Appointment date =
(Shipment Date - 1)
                              If Round(Now +
Reservation Lead Time) Start Time Slots = Preferred Start
Time then
If Round(Previous Appointment End Time) Start Time Slot =<
Preferred Start Time then
If Round(Next Appointment Start Time) Start Time Slot >=
Preferred Start Time then
If Preferred Start Time + Load Time =< Next Appointment Start
Time then
Appointment Start Time = Preferred Start Time
ElseIf Round(Previous Appointment End Time) Start Time Slot +
Load Time =< Next Appointment Time then
Appointment Start Time = Round(Previous Appointment End Time)

EndIf
                                              EndIf

                                    EndIf
```

```
If Round(Now + Reservation Lead Time) Start Time Slots >=
Previous Appointment End Time then
If Round(Previous Appointment End Time) Start Time Slot + Load
Time =< Next Appointment Start Time then
Appointment Start Time = Round(Now + Reservation Lead Time)
Start Time Slots

EndIf
                                                    EndIf

                                        EndIf

                            Endif

                  End if

            End if
            Exit if appointment found
pre date tolerance(i) = pre date tolerance(i) - 1
End if

Else
            No Appointment Possible
EndIf
EndIf
```

Notes: Some of the keywords used in this pseudo program are constraints as defined in the engine. Then we have transaction data from shipment record, pseudo code statements or functions, and objectives of the logic.

You can see that the logic is very complex and is very difficult to test. Creating test cases to test logic of this module requires deep domain expertise. It is very important to first break any complexity you encounter. After that, tackle the complexity at smaller levels at these smaller parts. Once you have complexity conquered at a smaller level, you can assemble all the parts to tackle the big complexity.

3.3 Technology Management

In the fast-changing world, technology is both a facilitator and a risk. New technology innovations help to do many tasks that were not possible earlier. At the same time, technology brings in some risks. From the perspective of a test professional, you need to test security aspects of the software application under test more rigorously, as now hackers have access to more powerful tools due to advancement in technology.

With the introduction of new technology at increasing speed, existing technology becomes obsolete very fast. You, as a test professional, need to test applications built using new technology; this is a challenge, as you will have to learn and understand this technology to test it. You, as a test professional, always have to keep an eye on the new technologies being developed and will have to keep upgrading your skills to be productive in your profession. On projects where you need to test such software applications, your penchant for learning new technologies will come in handy.

The testing tools need to be upgraded to be used successfully to test this new technology. Often it takes time before tool vendors release new versions that are capable of testing this new technology. In such instances, you need to look for alternative tools in the market which can offer this functionality. The test team will also need to upgrade their skills fast and should be adaptable to adjust to new demands.

If you are a test manager, then you will need to devise an appropriate strategy on your project so that demands for new technology and new tools can be met. Before the start of the project, make sure that you have taken the right initiatives to fulfill these demands on the project.

3.4 People Management

All software development activities are labor intensive and so are software testing activities. Never underestimate resource requirements for your project. At the same time, you must also evaluate to fit the right people for the right jobs. Not all people with the same skill sets are the same. So after seeing and evaluating all the testing tasks, decide which resources will be the right people for each of these tasks.

In life most people are not satisfied with their jobs because the assignments they get are not challenging. People get bored and unmotivated when they keep doing the same tasks again and again. To stimulate them, consult them often and provide opportunities for them to work on assignments that they think are challenging for them. Before assigning, also make sure that the person is capable of doing that assignment. Motivated people are always more productive than those who are not motivated. You can make your team more productive by providing them with opportunities to work on challenging assignments.

3.5 Skills Required

You will always find that skills required for the project and skills available to you are never the same. But you need to manage the project anyway. The best strategy is to first find available skills and then try to find how they will fit closely with which required skills. Once you have fitted closely fitting skills, you should think about how to cope with skills for which there are no properly matching skills available. Write these down. Once again, see your list of available skills. Try to match which skills are widely matching. To fill the gap in skill levels, you may need to arrange for some amount of training. After this exercise, you still will be left with skills that have no matching available skills. In all such cases you may be required either to hire additional staff or to provide complete training to existing staff who will work on those assignments.

3.6 Risk Factors

OK! So you have made a good plan that seems to be perfect. You have taken care of technical, people, and customer aspects that can impact your project. But in real life, most unexpected things can happen. Just yesterday the U.S. economy seemed to be chugging along strongly. Those big and blue corporations seemed infallible. But today the biggest and mightiest corporations have fallen flat on their bellies. The fall is so huge that the biggest economy in the world is shaking and it is going to change the world of business forever.

This kind of earth-shattering fate can happen with your project. So it is very important that you evaluate all kinds of risks before making your plan. Identify each and every risk that can impact your project. Make suitable (even more than suitable will be appropriate here!) allowances for each of these risks. These risks can be broadly categorized as technological risks, human risks, scheduling risks, etc.

To understand some of the risk aspects, let us look at a case study.

There is a software vendor who makes software that is used by big retailers in the United States for managing their back office, stores, and flow of goods and information with suppliers and customers. The application is built on the latest technology.

3.6.1 Technological Risks

Suppose the application you are going to test involves testing a Web-based Java application as well as testing its integration with a mobile module. The mobile module has a component that depends on information about tracking location of the truck using a GPS (Global Positioning System) service. What technological factors should be considered risks for testing this mobile module?

Here is a list:

1. Does a suitable mobile emulator exist which will help in testing this module?
2. Can this mobile emulator be installed successfully on your existing hardware and operating platform?
3. Does your testing team have prior experience in testing such mobile modules?
4. Does the main application integrate successfully with this mobile emulator? Is data flowing both ways between the main application and the emulator?
5. Does testing also involve getting real geographic coordinates data on the mobile and then finding its location based on this data? If this is the case, then this test case will need to be tested by using an actual mobile handset and getting real geographic coordinates data on it using any GPS service.

3.6.2 Scheduling Risk

1. Does your team need any training for testing this module?
2. Can you identify the kind of training required?
3. Is this training provided by any training service provider? How much time is needed for training?
4. Include this training time in your project estimates.

3.6.3 Human Risks

1. Can your team test this mobile module? Will you need to recruit new employees/contractors for this testing task?
2. If you need to recruit new people, then you may have to create a recruitment plan and include it in your testing plan.

3.7 Strategy for Automation

Traditionally the ROI for automation works out when any test case has to be executed more than 13 times. After this number of executions, automation works out to be cheaper than manual testing. For example, suppose for any test case that the total effort in writing the test case comes in at 15 minutes and manual execution needs 15 minutes. So the total time required for executing this test case 13 times is 6.5 hours. Now automation requires around 6 hours of work. Automated script for the test case runs in barely 3 minutes. So the time required for writing the test case, automating the test case, and running it 13 times is around 6 hours and 54 minutes. Sanity checks, performance checks, and some other tests that are run against production instance of any system are the best candidates for automation. Production environments do not change often, and on average some patches may be applied twice per year. This means that they are the most stable systems against which automation scripts may not have to be changed often. Most organizations run these sanity checks on a nightly basis to ensure that the production systems are running smoothly; if any problem occurs, then it is caught in the nightly run of the sanity check and the problem is fixed quickly before users start using the system in the office hours.

When a system is being built, many features are being added in future releases. Whenever any defects are found in previous releases, they are also fixed in the next release or a patch. Regression of existing features is tested in all of these next releases or patches. Whenever those features are touched upon in these new releases, they should be regression tested. So most of the features get tested again and again. So regression testing is also a good candidate for automation. In fact, the number of regression tests increases over time with new releases. But testing resources are limited and do not increase over time. So you end up having fewer resources for executing these regression tests. That is why it makes sense to automate them so that resource requirements can be reduced significantly.

3.8 Strategy for Manual Testing

Do you think that because you have automation experts and tools at your disposal, 100% of your testing should be automated? A big no! Automation is for repeated execution of test cases, which are in most cases for system sanity checks (in production instances) or for regression (in the case of new versions). In no way are they capable of breaking the system apart. Manual tests do exactly that. Domain experts use their experience to test workflows, integration touch points, and other functional aspects of the application to check if the system breaks.

Automating regression and sanity tests free these domain experts to concentrate on the kinds of testing that only human beings can do and require a lot of intuitive thinking.

Providing ample scheduled time and resources for manual testing will ensure a better and more effective software test effort.

3.9 Automation Tool Selection

Depending on the kind of project and its requirement, you will have to choose appropriate automation tools. But just because you have tools at your disposal does not mean that you are ready to go. Tools you bought are like a treadmill. Just because you bought the treadmill does not mean that you can lose weight. You will have to work out on the treadmill to lose weight. Similarly you need expert automation engineers who can use the tool to give you automated test scripts.

Nowadays many extremely popular portals are being developed and run by companies. Some of the most popular ones include Google, Yahoo, Microsoft Network, and Rediff. The numbers of users at such sites run in the millions. Supporting such a huge number of users is critical; the response time for these sites should be under acceptable limits. If your project is a Web-based application and it will be used not only by users at your customer company but also by outside people, then it is likely that you will need to test the application for performance against many concurrent users. So you may end up testing performance, stress, and load.

Depending on the life cycle phases of testing, you may need to test the application for sanity, regression, exploratory, and smoke.

There are many methodologies and tools available for automation of these functional tests. You should choose the right tools to suit your needs.

3.10 Strategy for Creating Automation Framework

Before thinking about automation, you will have to think about an easy way to maintain your automation scripts and test data and what kind of test cases are to be automated. Blindly automating everything or not thinking about maintenance work that will be required on your scripts will create problems for you later.

Automation frameworks allow you to tackle issues like maintenance and portability of your automation scripts. Automation framework will involve things like keywords creation, reusable code libraries creation, test data creation, and so on. Some amount of manual coding will be needed to do these tasks. You need to assess if your team consists of good automation engineers as well as domain experts who will create keywords, reusable libraries, and so on.

3.11 Software Product Life Cycle and Automation

Any product goes through different stages in its life from inception to design, production, testing, and finally product death. This is known as product life cycle (PLC). A lot of work is involved in getting the product through this life cycle. Through the last 50 years of software development and software testing, a lot has been learned and many processes have been refined and fine-tuned and many methodologies have been successfully adopted. However, the way to link automation effort with the rest of the software project will greatly differ from project to project or from one company to another company.

Manual operations at many organizations, whether manufacturing or service-related activities, have been successfully automated using computers or electronics. At factories robots, electronic devices, and computers are used to control manufacturing equipment to reduce operations costs substantially. In addition to the workplace, everyday life has become more comfortable and cheaper due to use of these devices. Computers and electronic devices are now so prevalent in everyday use, both at workplaces and in personal life, that we cannot think of our lives without these devices.

Coming to software testing, can we automate our software testing? It will mean using a software program to test a software program. Will it make sense? How can we integrate automation into a software testing project?

Here is a good solution. We can use a keyword-driven automation framework and link test phases with software development phases (see Figure 3.1;

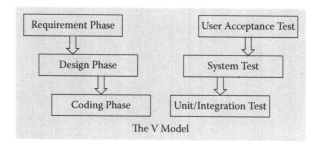

Figure 3.1 The V-Model.

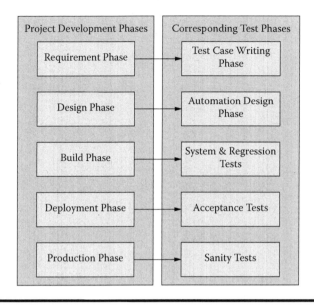

Figure 3.2   Software development phases and corresponding test phases.

keyword-driven automation frameworks are discussed in detail in Chapter 9.4 of this book).

In the V-Model, the requirement phase is linked to the User Acceptance Test, the design phase is linked to the System Test, and the build phase is linked to the Unit and Integration Test. But this model does not describe exactly when test design, test case writing, and test case execution should take place. It also fails to integrate automation-related activities of automation framework creation, script design, and script creation in the model.

So here is a modified model that removes these shortcomings of the V-Model (see Figure 3.2).

Referring to the figure, you can see that there is a matching phase for software testing to each software development phase. In fact, these phases are not corresponding but rather subsequent phases. So the requirement phase leads to the test case writing phase in software testing. The software requirement specifications document is the input for test case writing. The output of the design document is the input for the test automation design phase. Here you create your keyword framework, create automation scripts, and create your test data. After the build phase, you can create the test environment and start executing your system, regression, performance, and other tests. Here there will be iterations as the development team fixes reported defects and the test team verifies the fixes. Once these tests and fixes iterations are over, the system is handed over to the deployment team. Once deployment is done, the test team runs sanity tests and performance tests daily or at less frequent intervals depending on user requirements. In the production phase for fixing any defect there could be many possibilities. If the application is licensed and deployed inside the firewall, then if you have purchased support for the application from the software vendor, either the reported defect will be fixed by the vendor or they may suggest a work-around solution. If it is fixed, then the vendor will send a patch and you will have to apply the patch. If the application is a hosted application by the vendor, then they will apply the patch themselves.

3.12   Test Case Prioritization

Testing involves testing all functionality of the application as per test coverage. This includes trivial functionality of the application to the most important functionality of the application. Therefore it makes sense to prioritize your testing so that important functions are tested first and trivial functionality is tested later.

3.13   Ad Hoc Testing

Many times there is not much time available to make comprehensive planning for testing. This is true in an environment where quick new releases are the norm and everybody is pressed for time. Then, in other cases, there are smaller testing projects that may not require elaborate planning and have to be delivered quickly so that the team can move on to some bigger projects. In such situations ad hoc project planning can be employed. But ad hoc testing should be done only by people who are well versed in the application. In cases when software testing is outsourced and the team there is new for testing this application, ad hoc testing should never be employed.

3.14   Software Test Project Strategy Checklist

- ■ Have you included strategy for complexity management?
- ■ Have you included strategy for technology management?
- ■ Have you included strategy for people management?
- ■ Have you included strategy for skills management?
- ■ Have you included strategy for risk management?
- ■ Have you included strategy for automation?
- ■ Have you included strategy for manual testing?
- ■ Have you included strategy for automation tool selection?
- ■ Have you included strategy for creating automation framework?
- ■ Have you included strategy for executing test cases?
- ■ Have you included strategy for analysis and reporting?

3.15 Challenges

From the end user's perspective, it does not matter what methodology, tools, and strategies you are using for testing the software application as long as you achieve the target of delivering them a software application that is defect-free, has good performance even during peak loads, has good usability features, and works overall as intended and as per their expectations. They may forgive you for a late delivery but will never forgive you for delivering an application that fails in any of these goals. On the other hand, your customer's management will be looking at meeting costs and time deadlines for the project along with quality.

When testing project execution starts, management and end users may expect to receive timely and detailed reports so that they have a good understanding of project progress. The consideration here is that because they do not have access to what is going on with the project, they want a good report so that they are aware of the progress on the project.

3.16 Conclusion

It is an accepted fact that familiarity ensures better quality during product development. In the development of any product, the more time the development team spends on developing the product, the more mature and better the finished product is. To cut development time, standardized processes are adopted so that most of the activities related to the project have known courses of action. Similarly lessons learned from past projects ensure reduction of chances that any phase or activity of the project may go in the wrong direction, which may lead to higher costs, project delays, or bad product quality. In the case of software development, adherence to software engineering methodologies ensures reduced risks of defects entering in the software product.

On the other hand, introduction of the test team in the project from as early a stage as possible ensures a better percentage of error detection. The test team gets familiar with the product features and gets thoroughly familiar with the requirements. This ensures that the test team develops more understanding about the product and requirements. They have more time to make more iterations of testing with the product, which results in a better-tested product.

Chapter 4

Project Effort Estimation

Arguably in any project plan, effort estimation is the most difficult proposition. It is even more difficult for service providers. For bidding purposes, they make an initial project effort estimate based on initial customer requirements. At this stage, not many aspects of the project are crystal clear. Understanding about the project is also still not there. Most of the understanding about a project is gained only after a project starts getting executed. So effort estimation done at this stage is very crude and needs to be refined later.

Let us face it! Any service provider's life hinges on good effort estimation. If he is not able to come up with a good estimate, then he is going to lose money on that project. At the same time he must justify the efforts to the customer.

For making a quick effort estimate at the bidding stage, project managers use some formulas to arrive at a reasonable estimate. That is why there are so many formula-based effort estimation techniques available out there. They also use their experience and estimates from previous similar projects.

Even at a later stage when there is good clarity about the project, effort estimation can never be 100% accurate. Whereas the initial estimate at bidding level should be in the range of ±20% of the actual final effort, the estimate done at project strategy level should be ±10% of the actual final effort. If your estimate comes in these ranges, then you are in the comfort zone.

Any project needs to have detailed and well-defined time, quality, and cost estimates before the start of the project so that the project can be tracked any time during the project execution. For time estimates, time duration for each task in the project has to be defined and, through the use of PERT/CPM methods, total duration for the project can be estimated. Here it is assumed that many tasks are done in parallel. Many tasks are interlinked with each other, and some tasks cannot start before some other task is finished.

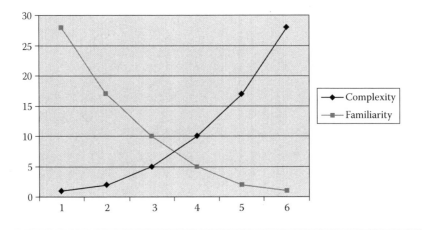

Figure 4.1   Effort for complexity vs. familiarity.

Any project has a lot of complexity. The bigger the project, the more complex it is. In fact, complexity rises faster than rise in project size. This is especially true for software testing projects. The greater the complexity, the greater will be the effort required. So complexity plays a very important part in effort estimation. You must define effort types for this reason. More complex parts need more effort, and less complex parts need less effort. Here it is interesting to know that familiarity also plays a vital role in effort estimation. For instance, a complex part may be familiar to the team, as they may have worked on similar assignments in the past and so are very familiar with this task. In this case, effort will be much less than if the team was not familiar with the task. So for effort estimation it is also a good idea to create a matrix based on complexity and familiarity with each part of the project.

As you can see in Figure 4.1, as complexity increases, effort increases steeply, whereas as familiarity increases, effort decreases steeply. That is why it is better to hire experienced people on the project even at substantially higher salaries than to hire inexperienced people at a fraction of that salary.

4.1   Estimation by Experience

Experience no doubt plays an important role in effort estimation. Even in so-called objective calculation of effort estimation, all aspects are not completely objective and a certain percentage of subjective assessment goes in. And that is where experience counts. In fact, based on experience the entire effort can be calculated to a certain degree of accuracy without requiring any help from statistical methods. Some of the areas in objective effort calculation methods such as test point analysis (TPA) where subjective assessments creep in include calculation for productivity and test strategy. Even project sizing calculations cannot be said to be entirely based on objective assessment.

In any case, even after calculating effort by any method, it should be thoroughly checked by somebody who has experience in effort estimation. Only then can the accuracy of the effort calculation be certified. No alternatives have been found for experience when it comes to effort estimation!

4.2 Estimation Using Test Point Analysis

Software products and applications are built using well-defined smaller components. Each component is integrated with other components through interfaces. These interfaces have the facility of input/output so that the component can communicate with other components. For TPA, functions with which the software application has been built are used as the basic point to calculate the effort estimate.

Function point analysis is a sound technique used for estimating effort for software development projects. TPA is built on the basis of function point analysis and is a very good technique for effort estimation for test projects. TPA can be used to prepare an estimate for a system test or acceptance test. TPA covers only black box testing and is not meant to estimate effort for white box testing (unit/integration testing done by developers). Effort estimates for white box testing are taken care of in the function point analysis itself. TPA is also used to determine the relative importance of the various functions in comparison to each other and on the basis of the entire project. This helps in using the available testing time as efficiently as possible. In essence, TPA is an objective way to determine effort estimation for test projects.

4.2.1 Basic Components of TPA

TPA calculations are based on three characteristics of the project: the size of the software application to be tested, the test strategy (test coverage, quality standards, and complexity of components under test), and the level of productivity. While productivity of resources varies from resource to resource and from organization to organization, size and test strategy determine the volume of work to be performed. This volume is expressed in terms of the number of test points. Multiplying this volume with productivity will determine the number of hours of test activities to be performed.

4.2.1.1 Project Size

When any project is to be initiated, project sizing is the first element that is determined. You will already have project development size information (number of function points) available from function point analysis that is done by the development team. You will then have to research additional information in order to find the number of test points. Specifically, you will need to research complexity, number of interfaces, and uniformity of components to be tested. Here complexity refers to the number of conditions (loops, conditional statements, etc., in a function). If a software component consists of many conditions or conditions with many steps (many loops or conditional statements), then that component will definitely need to be tested for these large conditions, resulting in more test cases for testing that component. This translates into a greater volume of work to be performed. The number of interfaces refers to the number of parameters that pass into or out of a function to another function. A greater number of interfaces means more testing effort, as interfaces are the integration points between functions, and testing work should include testing of these interfaces to ensure that data is getting passed from one function to anther correctly. If a software application consists of similar functions, then the volume of testing work gets reduced. On the contrary, if the software application consists of a number of functions that are very different from each other, the volume of testing work gets increased substantially. This factor is known as uniformity.

4.2.1.2 Test Strategy

In the contract agreement, the customer should have specified quality requirements for the application under test. At the project strategy level, granularity of test activities must be determined to ensure that these quality standards are met. These quality standards should also include quality norms at the subsystem/component level. These norms and standards will determine the thoroughness of the test activities based on the granularity level required. Also, different quality parameters to be adhered to will influence the volume of test activities. Test coverage required for each component is one such factor that greatly influences volume of work. Test coverage is directly related to intensity of usage of any function by users. These aspects should be discussed with the customer to arrive at effort estimation keeping in view of these aspects. Perspectives of different stakeholders also influence volume of test work. Some functionalities of the application under test may be used extensively by a set of users and are considered critical by them, whereas some other functionalities of the application under test are seldom used by anyone. Definitely thoroughness and quality of testing will differ in these two situations, and thus testing effort will be different. It is very important for the test team to identify such scenarios and estimate their volume of work accordingly.

4.2.1.3 Productivity

In TPA, productivity relates to the time necessary to complete the tasks associated with one test point. Productivity consists of two components. One is the skill and experience level of the person doing a task. The other component is the environment factor that influences this productivity level. An environment factor could be usage of productivity or automation tools and experience of the test team in using these tools. Thus we can see that productivity varies from person to person, from team to team, and from organization to organization. The more productive the test team is, the less the effort will be and vice versa.

4.2.2   TPA Calculation Details

TPA calculation is a complex task at best. But I will try to make it as simple as possible. I will also try to make it short.

TPA calculation consists of knowing the number of function points and the type of these function points.

Sometimes function point information may not be available to the test manager. In such instances, he will have to make a rough estimate of the number of function points in the system so that he can calculate his TPA. One method is to count the number of logical conditions/interfaces and multiply this figure by 30.

So,

Number of function points = number of logical conditions × 30

4.2.2.1   Dynamic Test Point Characteristics

Dynamic test points are influenced by many factors. These factors can be categorized as function and quality requirements dependent. Quality requirements factors are further dependent on usage intensity and quality level. Quality requirements are derived from the test strategy factors. As is obvious, usage intensity is a factor that denotes how much a function will be used by end users. Some functions may be sparingly used while some functions may be extensively used by end users. For calculations, a general rule is that 25% of functions can be considered as having high, 50% as medium, and 25% as low usage intensity. Quality level is the factor that determines to what extent the whole application will be tested. For general-purpose applications not requiring transactions and where end users do not expect a high level of reliability, software testing can be up to moderate level and no extensive testing may be required. But for applications requiring a high level of reliability (i.e., a mission-critical application with transactions), software testing should be done extensively to uncover and fix as many critical defects as possible.

With regard to function-related factors, there are three factors in this category: interfacing, uniformity, and complexity. Interfacing is a factor that is influenced by logical data sets, which in fact are the number of points of contact (parameters) with other functions. The more parameters a function has through which data passes, the more weightage it has for interfacing. The uniformity factor denotes how much functions in an application differ from each other. This is done by counting how many functions are similar to a standard function in the system. The complexity factor denotes how many functions in an application can be considered complex from observing the conditional statements inside those functions. If conditional statements are large with many conditions, that function will be considered complex.

To calculate dynamic test point, usage intensity, quality level, interfacing, and complexity are added and then this figure is multiplied by the uniformity factor. This figure then divided by 16 gives the dynamic test point.

So,

$$DF = (UI + QL + IN + CM) * UN/16$$

where

$\qquad$ DF = dynamic test point
$\qquad$ UI = usage intensity
$\qquad$ QL = quality level
$\qquad$ IN = interfacing
$\qquad$ CM = complexity
$\qquad$ UN = uniformity

4.2.2.2 Dynamic Quality Characteristics

The quality of any software system can be defined in terms of reliability, efficiency, robustness, suitability, efficiency, security, usability, and so on. In TPA calculations, only four of them are considered: suitability, efficiency, security, and usability. Suitability signifies how much any system design conforms to the actual user requirements. Efficiency signifies how well a user can use its features without sacrificing speed of using the application. Security signifies how secure the application is against threat of data theft or unauthorized access. Usability signifies how well features are laid out on the screen to enhance the user experience. Many types of tests are used to find each of these quality characteristics.

So,

$$QD = ST * WT(ST) + EF * WT(EF) + SC * WT(SC) + US * WT(US)$$

where

$\qquad$ QD = quality characteristics for a function
$\qquad$ ST = suitability factor for the function
$\qquad$ EF = efficiency factor for the function
$\qquad$ SC = security factor for the function
$\qquad$ US = usability factor for the function

$\qquad$ WT(ST), WT(SC), WT(US), and WT(EF) are the weightage factors for suitability, security, usability, and efficiency factors for the function.

4.2.2.3   Test Point Calculation

Once we have all the data for function point characteristics and quality characteristics, test point calculation for each function can be done. The total number of test points is the sum of individual test points for each function.

So,

$$TP = FP * DF * QD$$

where

TP = number of dynamic test points assigned to a function
FP = number of function points assigned to the function
DF = weighing factor for the function dependent factors
QD = weighing factor for the dynamic quality characteristics

There is one more factor that is known as indirect quality characteristics. Basically some of the quality characteristics can be applied not at the function level but at the application level. This happens when measuring quality characteristics at the function level is not possible.

So the total number of test points (TTP) for the entire application can be given as

$$TTP = \Sigma TP + (FP * QI)/500$$

where

TPA = total number of test points assigned to the application as a whole
ΣTP = sum of the dynamic test points assigned to the individual functions
FP = total number of function points assigned to the system as a whole
QI = weighing factor for the indirectly measurable quality characteristics

4.2.2.4   Productivity Factor

In TPA calculation, test strategy and application size information comes from the customer. But productivity comes from the team that will be doing the testing. If the test team has good exposure to test tools, has good knowledge, and has good experience and the environment in which they are working is good, then the team will have good productivity. So they will be able to test the application faster. If a team has lower productivity, then they will take more time to test the same application. So the productivity factor can vary from one organization to the next or from one organizational unit to the next unit. Productivity for any organization or unit can best be calculated from historical data if it is available. So many customers make it a point during negotiation to know how the testing team had performed on previous projects so that they can estimate how fast the testing team can test the application.

Environment factors also play a vital role in productivity apart from personal factors of the members of the test team. Test tools allow the test team to either do testing quickly or manage the testing activity better. Development testing specifies what kind of information is available for testing done at the previous level. Test basis is the factor that specifies the documentation level for the project. Development environment factor specifies the development environment used for developing the application. So an application developed using a modern language like Java will take less time in developing the application than using a procedural language like Pascal or COBOL. Test environment factor specifies the test bed preparation factor. Testware factor is the availability of existing test cases, automation scripts, and so on.

The environmental factor (E) is calculated by adding together the ratings for the various environmental variables (test tools, development testing, test basis, development environment, test environment, and testware) and then dividing the sum by 21 (the sum of the nominal ratings). Normally, one environmental factor is worked out for the system as a whole, but separate factors can be calculated for the individual subsystems if appropriate.

4.2.2.5 Primary Test Hours

Once we have the total number of tests for the entire application, we can find out testing hours required. While total number of test points will provide the volume of test work to be done, the productivity factor will determine at what speed this volume of work can be done. Multiplying these two will give the number of test hours to be spent to test the application.

The number of primary test hours is obtained by multiplying the number of test points by the productivity factor:

$$TH = TTP * PR$$

where
  TH = the total number of primary test hours
  TTP = the total number of test points for the system
  PR = the productivity factor

4.2.2.6 Total Number of Test Hours

Primary test hours information provides how many test hours are needed for testing the application. Now we need to add management hours spent on the project for planning, monitoring, reporting, and controlling the project to get total hours to be spent on the project. Generally management hours are given as 10% of primary test hours. If there are more layers of management for the project, management hours will be more.

4.2.2.7 Phase Breakdown

As can be seen, the TPA calculation is done at the project level. So from TPA we have effort estimate and number of hours required for planning, controlling, and doing testing. But effort estimates for different phases of the project cannot be derived from this calculation. To get effort and number of hours of work required for different phases of the project, we need to divide this figure to get hours and effort required in each phase. There is no well-established formula for doing so. The test manager can make an estimate and then divide the total effort into these phases.

4.2.3 Application of TPA

TPA is a somewhat objective method of calculating effort estimation. But it is very complicated. It requires elaborate sets of data on which complex calculations are done to arrive at the solution. Not many people use TPA with this many detailed calculations. At the majority of places, test managers use approximate values for TPA. This is because all the needed data may not be available to the test manager. Furthermore, doing all these complex calculations takes a lot of time.

Some aspects of TPA cannot be claimed to be truly objective. For instance, productivity measurement is done based on historical data. Even size and test strategy measurements cannot be said to be truly objective, contrary to claims.

TPA is widely used for providing some initial effort estimate at the bidding stage.

4.2.4 TPA at Bidding Stage

Service providers need a good tool to provide an effort estimate for a project at the bidding stage. The effort estimate is one of the most important criteria for any service provider to win a bid. At the same time, if he underestimates his bid substantially from what could be the actual effort during execution, then he runs the risk of losing money. For this reason he must have a good tool for a rough initial effort estimate. TPA comes in handy in this respect.

Until detailed functional specifications are obtained, however, it is not possible to determine factors such as complexity, interfacing, and so on. Nevertheless, a rough function point analysis can be performed on the basis of very general specifications. If a rough function point count is available, a rough TPA can be estimated.

For a rough TPA, a single function is defined whose size is determined by the total function point count. All function-dependent factors (quality level, usage intensity, complexity, interfacing, and uniformity) are usually assigned a normal value. A TPA can then be carried out as described in previous paragraphs.

4.3   TPA-Based Effort Estimation Implementation

You will find many techniques from universities, research organizations, training institutes, and other sources, but mind you, they are more of a theoretical nature and may not have practical significance. You may not be able to practice them in your on-the-job assignments, as they may lack something that constitutes the difference between theory and practice.

Effort estimation for software test projects is difficult because test projects comprise many different kinds of tasks. You have functional testing, automation testing, automation scripts, performance testing, security testing, compatibility testing, and so on. The approach for estimating effort for each of these tasks is different.

Many organizations and individuals have made efforts to create a standard approach for making effort estimation for these tasks. But no single approach has ever become a standard model. That is why there are so many estimation techniques out there and organizations use their own method of estimation depending on their needs and convenience.

However, one practical technique that is being used by many software services companies is presented here. Basically this approach is based on the TPA model. First, identify each activity or task in the project. Then, estimate the effort for each of these tasks. Finally, sum up effort estimates for these tasks. This will be the total effort required for the entire project.

Test effort may differ from one project to another; nevertheless, the same technique can be used for effort estimation.

Here are the steps for estimation:

1. Identify different stages of the test life cycle
2. Identify all the activities for each test life cycle
3. Estimate size for each phase
4. Estimate effort for each phase
5. Estimate effort for regression cycle
6. Compute total testing effort

4.3.1   Identify Test Life Cycle Stages

Of course the testing effort for a project can be conveniently divided into different stages. With process standardization over the years, the following software testing life cycle stages are the most commonly used these days:

1. Test requirement
2. Test case design
3. Test script development
4. Test case execution
5. Test result analysis and documentation

Most of the test requirements can be deduced from the software requirement specifications documents. In the test case design phase, both manual and automated test cases are identified and generated. If you are using any keyword-driven automation framework, then in the design phase you also develop the keyword library. In the test script development phase, automated test scripts are generated using either the automated test tool or manually programming or a combination of both. The test execution phase involves executing both manual and automated test cases. The test result analysis and documentation phase involves analyzing the result and reporting the defects. In fact, if the number of test cases is not huge, then the test case execution phase and test result analysis phase can be combined.

The objective of identifying different life cycles is to estimate size and effort for each phase and document the estimation assumption for each phase. Later on, the team can work back on the estimation for variation in estimation.

4.3.2   Identify Activities for Each Phase

The main focus of this activity is to identify the activities involved in each phase of the test life cycle. The job of the testing team is to estimate the size of the activities in terms of man-hours. During each test phase activities will result in documents for that phase. So we will have test planning and strategy documents after the test requirements phase, test and scenario cases and keywords after the test case generation phase, automation scripts after the test automation phase, and a test log after the test analysis phase.

4.3.3   Size Estimation for Each Phase

The main focus of this activity is to estimate the size of the activities for each phase. While estimating the size for each phase, all the assumptions considered during estimation should be documented for future analysis if any variation in estimation exists. The Wide Band Size Estimation technique can be used to do size estimation for each phase. Also the Historical Project Database can be made available to the testing team as a reference depending on the project scope and nature. Size estimation for each phase is detailed below.

4.3.3.1   Test Requirement Phase

In this phase we estimate the number of scenarios required from analyzing the project requirement and identifying the number of scenarios required based on the test strategy. The testing team should brainstorm the project requirement and categorize the test requirement. The Wide Band Delphi Technique (a heuristic approach to effort estimation where different estimates from different people for the same task are averaged out to make a single final estimate) can be used to estimate the number of test requirements.

Test requirement can be categorized as follows:

- Functional
- Performance
- Security
- Integration with other systems
- Compatibility

Also the testing team should identify the positive and negative test requirement for each category. This will help the testing team in identifying the test data. The purpose of this activity is to make the testing team part of the estimation for the test requirement stage. Also, any ambiguity in the requirement can also be addressed at this stage.

The size estimation process for the test requirement phase begins with taking the inputs that are project requirements and use cases from the design documents. Project requirements are analyzed to identify the number of scenarios required to cover all requirements for each category. So we have a number of scenarios for each category by this time.

4.3.3.2 Test Case Design Phase

In this phase we estimate the number of test cases required. Both manual and automated test cases are identified in this phase. Also test data are identified for positive and negative condition. The design of test case is based on the test strategy.

The inputs for the size estimation process for test case design are the scenarios for all categories. Each scenario is analyzed to find the number of test cases to cover each scenario. For each category of testing, the number of test cases is derived. Estimation assumptions are also recorded for future reference. By this stage we will have a good idea about the total number of functional, performance, security, integration, and compatibility test cases.

Sometimes within different scenarios there may be the same test cases. These same test cases can be clubbed to avoid duplication.

4.3.3.3 Test Script Development Phase

In this phase we estimate the total number of automated test cases using automated test tools. The test tool will generate test script. These generated scripts must be modified as per automation framework deployed. The goal of the estimation team is to identify the number of test scripts and lines of code (LOC).

Size estimation for the test script development phase consists of estimating the number of test cases to be automated. Out of all test cases, the number of integration test cases and data-driven test cases are estimated. In each test case, how many checkpoints are to be inserted? How many test cases will need testing with external interfaces? The selected automation framework will determine if script components can be reused. For instance, if a keyword-driven framework is chosen, then there will not be any repetition of any component. A keyword will identify each component. Now we can estimate LOC from the number of test scripts.

4.3.3.4   Test Case Execution Phase

In this phase we estimate the number of manual and automated test cases to be executed. The output of this phase is the test log. We count the number of manual and automated test cases and make estimates as to how much time it will take to execute all test cases. We also estimate the probable number of defects that can be identified.

4.3.3.5   Regression Phase

If we are working on projects where we have to deal with software with many versions, then we have to do regression testing to make sure that in the new versions of the software existing features are still functional. The test team is responsible for identifying which test cases will be run in each regression cycle. Also the team needs to identify how many manual and automated test cases will be run in each regression cycle.

4.3.4   Effort Estimation for Each Phase

Based on the size estimated for each stage of testing phase, the total testing effort for the project can be calculated as follows:

Total effort of each phase = Size of the total activities × Productivity

The productivity factor should be considered separately for manual and automated testing.

Productivity is specific to the organization, as it is influenced by the knowledge and skill level of the testing team. For automated testing activity, the productivity factor is influenced by the knowledge and skill level of the testing team. In fact, productivity will be influenced by a lot of factors, such as the following:

- Type of application—Web based, stand-alone, or client/server.
- Automation tools used—Some tools work directly as application level (e.g., Worksoft's tool captures business logic of SAP systems without any manual programming; some tools need a lot of manual modification). These factors deeply influence productivity.
- Automation framework used—If a good automation framework is used, then maintenance required for different releases for regression and sanity scripts will be low, which will result in higher productivity.

So productivity may vary from place to place. Now let us take one example for calculating effort required in test case generation, script generation, and test case execution for both manual testing and automation testing.

Let us see how we can calculate effort estimation for the entire project including functional testing, regression testing, integration testing, and so on.

$$\text{Total effort for manual test case generation (A)} = \text{Number of manual test cases} \times \text{Productivity}$$

$$\text{Total effort for manual test case execution (B)} = \text{Number of manual test cases} \times \text{Productivity}$$

where Productivity = Number of test cases executed/Time.

Similarly, for automated test cases we can compute effort required for test case generation. But in this case we also have to compute effort required to create script. So in the case of automated test cases,

$$\text{Effort required to generate test case} + \text{script (C)} = \text{Number of test cases} \times \text{Productivity} + \text{Total LOC} \times \text{Productivity}$$

Similarly, the effort required to execute automated test cases (D) = number of test cases × productivity.

Summing all of them will give effort required for creation and execution of entire test cases for the project.

$$\text{Effort required for entire project (X)} = A + B + C + D$$

Apart from the test case writing, automation, and execution, we also have other efforts in the project. So we end up making effort estimates for planning effort, management effort, rework effort, and so on.

$$\text{Total project effort} = \text{Total testing effort} + \text{Regression testing effort} + \text{Planning effort} + \text{Management effort} + \text{Rework effort}$$

4.3.5 Synopsis

Effort estimation is a very important activity in any project. Budget, resource allocation, and project success will depend a lot on how good your effort estimate is. If your estimate is less than the effort eventually required, then you will not be able to get those extra resources, and in that case your project may be doomed to fail.

4.4   Importance of Effort Estimation

There are two aspects of effort estimation. One aspect is resources required for the project, and the other aspect is the schedule for the project. The amount of resources required directly relates to costs for your project. Schedule relates directly to customer satisfaction. If, due to a lower schedule estimate than actually required, your project gets delayed, then it adversely affects customer's confidence.

It is a reality that on most projects resource requirements increase as the project progresses. Similarly the schedule also gets prolonged with progress of the project. Customers will never be ready to accept these increases easily. So it is very important that from the beginning of the project you project schedule and resource requirements realistically.

On the other hand, you must justify your schedule and resource estimates to your customers. Every aspect of your estimate should reflect justifiable explanations. Projects with automation of test case execution always face a wrong expectation from customers. Customers expect that due to the automation element, project schedules should be collapsed. But in reality, the opposite is true. Automated test cases require the additional task of creating scripts, so a greater effort is required for automated test cases than for manual test cases. The benefit of automated test cases comes when they are executed. They take less time in execution compared to manual test cases. Also automation frameworks (e.g., keyword-driven automation frameworks) require effort to be created. But when they are in place, they reduce effort in maintaining automation scripts in different versions of the software, and they are extremely useful for regression test cases.

4.5   Practical Advice

Whatever techniques you will use for effort estimation, you will also have to consider the ground realities. This includes personal productivity of your team members. Even though software engineering processes mitigate this risk to some extent, it is still a very important input for your planning. Not all people have the same productivity when it comes to performing a task. Similarly, even with the same skill set, no two people can do the same tasks with the same output. Some may be good at performing a specific category of tasks. For instance, I had two guys with the same skill sets and the same level of experience. But one had an aptitude for doing simpler tasks and was very productive with those tasks. The other guy was never that productive with any task, but he was good analytically. So he could take complex tasks and do them without much difficulty. So the best strategy for me was to assign simpler tasks with more volume to the first guy and assign complex tasks to the other guy. Using these practical approaches, you can achieve more productivity from your team.

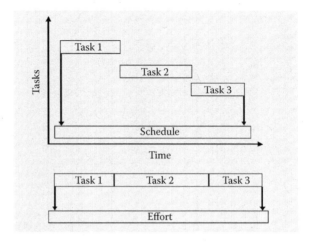

Figure 4.2 Schedule vs. effort in waterfall model.

4.6 Schedule versus Effort

In the waterfall model, each subprocess in software development strictly follows the preceding subprocess. The subsequent subprocess always starts after the preceding subprocess ends. That is why we tackle the design phase after the requirements phase has been completed, the coding phase after the design phase has been completed, and so on. So, in the waterfall model, the schedule is always equal to the effort for the project. Accordingly the software test processes also follow the strict regime that is followed by the development and design processes (see Figure 4.2).

In agile development, however, things are different. Subprocesses do not strictly follow the rule that the subsequent subprocess should start only after the preceding subprocess ends. Due to this, it can happen that a subprocess will start even if the preceding subprocesses are still being executed. Due to this, the effort can be different from the schedule. In such environments the schedule can be equal to or less than the effort for the project.

If your project has this requirement, then be prepared to calculate your effort and schedule accordingly (see Figure 4.3).

4.7 Task Elasticity

There is another aspect to schedule and effort. Some tasks can be completed faster either by increasing the loading factor of existing allocated resources or by adding more resources to the task (see Figures 4.4 and 4.5).

On the other hand, some tasks cannot be completed faster by adding more resources to the task. One example could be a small task that needs some amount of preparation. You must include the time required for preparation in your schedule.

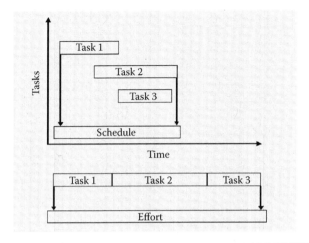

Figure 4.3 Schedule vs. effort in agile model.

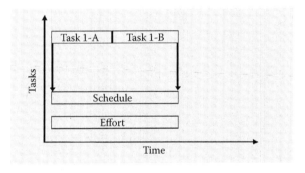

Figure 4.4 Dependent task parts and schedule and effort for task completion.

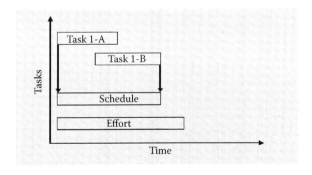

Figure 4.5 Independent task parts and schedule and effort for task completion.

If one person is assigned that task, then first he will do preparation for the task and then he will start working on the task. Suppose preparation requires 8 hours and the task requires 8 hours. If you assign two people for this task, then each person will take 8 hours for preparation. The task may be divided and each person may take 4 hours to complete his portion of the task. In the first case, it will take 16 hours (preparation time + task completion time). In the second case, it will take 12 hours if there is no dependency between the divided tasks. But if there is a dependency, then the task completion will still take 16 hours, as the dependent task cannot be started until the task on which this task depends completes.

So you see, even after adding resources, you cannot complete a task faster.

4.8   Effort Estimation Checklist

4.8.1   Checklist for Software Test Schedule Estimation

- Have test life cycle stages been identified?
- Have the activities for each phase been identified?
- Has size estimation for each phase been identified?
- Has size estimation for the test requirement phase been identified?
- Has size estimation for the test case design phase been identified?
- Has size estimation for the test script development phase been identified?
- Has size estimation for the test case execution phase been identified?
- Has schedule estimation for each phase been identified?
- Have size and schedule estimations for the regression cycle been made?
- Has schedule estimation for all kinds of testing (functional, performance, security, compatibility, integration, and any other type of testing) been done?

4.8.2   Checklist for Software Test Effort Estimation

- Have test life cycle stages been identified?
- Have the activities for each phase been identified?
- Has size estimation for each phase been identified?
- Has size estimation for the test requirement phase been identified?
- Has size estimation for the test case design phase been identified?
- Has size estimation for the test script development phase been identified?
- Has size estimation for the test case execution phase been identified?
- Has effort estimation for each phase been identified?
- Have size and effort estimations for the regression cycle been made?
- Has effort estimation for all kinds of testing (functional, performance, security, compatibility, integration, and any other type of testing) been done?

4.9 Challenges

Even when the most complete documentation is provided before the start of the project, it is very difficult to precisely estimate effort required. But as the project progresses, many unknown aspects of the project become clearer. More understanding is also developed among the team members over time. So the initial estimation may be wrong, and you may need to update this value and report it to stakeholders. At this time you may need to explain why some of the initial estimates were wrong. The guideline is that if a value is within 10% tolerance of the initial estimate, then it is OK. In cases when something drastic happens, your estimates can become totally wrong. In such cases you need to immediately report the discrepancy to stakeholders. Of course, it is real life and bizarre things can happen at any time.

There is one more aspect to effort estimation. For billing purpose or effort estimate for the project (fixed time – fixed budget), when you present your effort estimate to the customer, it makes sense if a standard approach is adopted to make that estimate. The standard estimates are derived from acceptable formulas like the ones used in TPA estimates. Even though some elements of these techniques are still subjective and vary from one estimate to another, customers will be more willing to accept them.

In any case, never commit more than you can deliver in time. Your motto should be "commit less and deliver more." It never should be "commit more and deliver less." This is the secret of successful test managers!

Chapter 5

Software Testing Project Plan

Any project should have four distinct parts: strategy, planning, execution, and reporting. Essentially at project strategy you will be evaluating your strengths and ways to find the best use of resources at your disposal against the set of requirements and tasks you are supposed to accomplish for the project.

In today's business world, outsourcing is a fact of life, especially so in the case of software development. Outsourced software projects are inherently different from in-house software projects. Accordingly project planning for these outsourced projects is also different. Offshoring adds another twist to already complex goings-on in these projects. Priorities for different stakeholders also get changed. To win contracts the outsourcing service providers have to come up with mature and proven project processes, technical expertise, domain expertise, and a proven track record.

During presales efforts the outsourcing service provider gets some input about the project from the customer and makes an initial assessment about effort estimation and an initial project plan. Once the project is bagged, then a detailed project plan is made for the project. In this book we will not discuss the project planning done at the presales level. We will concentrate only on the project planning done after the project is bagged and a detailed project plan is then done for the entire project.

Basically project strategy and effort estimation are done at a higher level. Once you have completed these tasks, you can move forward to detailed level planning, providing minute details about skills matching, actual resource allocation, actual tool selection, exact methodology to be deployed for kinds of testing to be performed, framework to be created for automation, and so on. These activities are done when you do your project planning.

5.1 Test Area Prioritization

Each resource allocated to your project has a workload that comprises priority areas and normal tasks. Priority tasks are the ones that deliver customer satisfaction and contribute to project success. So it is very important that resources perform these priority tasks first. This is especially true in the test case execution phase, where some test case results are vital and so should be prioritized to be executed ahead of other test cases. For instance, the customer may like to see early test results for some critical new features that have been added in the new release. In this case, test cases related to these features should be executed ahead of other test areas.

5.2 Skill Matching

Software test skills are getting more and more specialized along with software testing practice maturity. In the early days some 20 years back, a test team could have test managers, test engineers, team leaders, usability experts, and some other odd professionals on the test team. But not anymore! Now the team could have test managers, test analysts, domain experts, usability experts, delivery managers, test engineers, automation engineers, and so on. If your project is an outsourced one, then most probably your team must be following some form of TMM process. In some good organizations an elaborate process is followed to reduce test effort using a framework of the center of excellence model. So many people in your team may be working on more than one project simultaneously.

5.3 Resource Allocation

With pressure to reduce costs more and more, test teams are now facing the heat to deliver more and more in less time on their projects. So resource allocation plays a major role in achieving profitability for the outsourcing service provider on each of their projects. Thus, resource allocation does not impact just one project but has direct bearing on the bottom line of the outsourcing service provider. For this reason resource allocation for any upcoming project cannot be done in isolation. Many resources can be working on more than one project simultaneously. Thus, the time of each resource is very precious and their time for the new project should be utilized conservatively.

5.4 Tools Selection

Depending on project requirements, you may need to select tools for test case repository, automating test case execution, defect tracking, defect reporting, and so on. Different tools have different advantages and disadvantages over others. At the same time, your particular needs will dictate which particular tools from which vendor should be selected. One more important angle is that you should select tools that are familiar to your team so that each tool can be effectively used by everyone on the team. This will also reduce training needs for learning new tools.

5.5 Methodology Selection

There has been a lot of work on defining and refining software project management methodologies so that productivity, efficiency, and quality can be improved in software projects. In this respect some of the pioneering work has been done by the Software Engineering Institute at Carnegie Mellon University in Pittsburgh, Pennsylvania. They introduced Capability Maturity Model standards for software project processes for the entire software development life cycle (SDLC). These process improvement techniques have helped software development processes mature significantly and thus have helped to produce software systems with excellent quality.

But these standards have never touched upon processes that are used in software testing. For some time now, effort has been made to establish a similar standard for testing. It is currently known as the software testing life cycle (STLC). Here parallel and similar processes are defined compared to SDLC. Using it, organizations can improve upon efficiency and quality of the software.

5.6 Sample Project

A sample project is described here. Names of customer and testing service provider have been changed to protect their identities.

The client Super Nova Corporation is engaged in developing software applications for retailers, manufacturers, logistics service providers, and distributors. Using their application, clients could plan, execute, and monitor their entire supply chain systems in real time. Some of the major features of the system include appointment scheduling of trucks for delivery and receiving, yard management, warehouse management, transportation management, GPS integration for tracking of in-transit trucks in real time, truck load planning, route optimization, 3PL service provider management, inventory management, inventory visibility across the entire supply chain, forecasting, automatic order generation, order management, supplier management, cross-docking, vendor-managed inventory, drop shipment, individual calendars for all entities, and so on. For government regulation compliance as well as for business use, audit trail features maintain a history of all transactions.

Their application is being used by major U.S. and European companies as well as by some government departments. Using their application, organizations are able to manage their distribution centers, transportation of goods, retail outlets, and so on. Some of these organizations have sites in excess of 5000. At some organizations concurrent users could be in excess of 10,000.

5.6.1   Technology

The software is developed using Java with the latest technology like Ajax menu, rich browser user interface, and so on, for the application. The underlying workbench is an eclipse plug in which business workflows, navigation, menu architecture, feature turn on/turn off switches, linking roles to features, and so on, are defined which directly affect the resultant user interface, as the user interface is launched based on the configurations defined in the workbench.

5.6.2   Infrastructure

Geographically scattered teams were simultaneously working and developing the application. Some of the teams were from service providers who were working as offshore extensions of the core development team. Similarly testing teams were working from offshore locations. But all the code was compiled on one development server located in the United States. There is an automated smoke testing application using cruise control. Whenever any code is submitted to the development server, cruise control runs automatically and compiles the new code with the existing code base. If the new submitted code breaks the build, then cruise control throws a fail message and generates an error message, which it sends to registered e-mail addresses. Once the code breaks, the developer who checked the code in is also sent an automated e-mail containing the error and code break message. The developer then works to fix the problem and rechecks his code on the server. This process continues until a clean code is checked in and no error occurs and code compiles successfully. The error message will also be displayed on the online status page of cruise control. If the new code compiles cleanly with the existing code base, then a success message is thrown by cruise control.

For version control, CVS (Perforce) system is used. Whenever a new version of the software application is started, a new branch is created in the version control system. At any time there are more than 20 active branches and versions of the software. They have had more than 9 major and 90 minor releases of the software application since the application development started.

5.6.3   Testing Resources

For testing purposes UAT (user acceptance testing), pre-UAT (pre-user acceptance testing), and local builds are deployed on different machines. On any branch of the application, somewhere between 5 and 35 developers, project managers, business analysts, and software testers were working simultaneously.

Whenever development on a branch completed and the development team handed over the build to the testing team for testing, a pre-UAT mirror environment was created and testing commenced after due test planning and adoption of a sound project strategy.

5.6.4   Testing Process

Whenever a new version of the software or customer-specific implementation is done, the testing team verifies and validates the version using regression and system testing. The testing team gets involved when initial requirements and design are ready. The testing team reviews requirements and design. If there are any issues from a testing perspective, the team notifies the development team. Once the team is satisfied, it okays requirements and design. The test manager then does strategy, effort estimation, and planning for testing the version of the software.

Because the entire effort is in developing and testing the product, the development and testing cycles are short and iterative. This cycle is a perfect example of agile development. Documentation is minimal. Project managers, business analysts, the development team, and the testing team constantly communicate with each other through e-mails, instant messengers, live Internet demonstrations, and teleconferences. Through these communications geographically scattered teams perform knowledge transfer, issue resolution, brainstorming, status reporting, and other such tasks.

Once business analysts get customer requirements, they create and pass the customer-approved SRS document (software requirements specifications) to the testing and development teams. The software architect creates and passes mock-up documents to these teams. The mock-up document consists of UI screens that will be available to users along with the flow of events and workflows. This document is akin to the design document. Mostly these two documents become available to development and testing teams when customer-specific versions of the software application are to be released. The project manager estimates effort required and creates a project plan. He then assigns tasks to individual team members of the development team. Similarly the test manager makes testing effort estimates and creates a test plan. He then assigns tasks to individual test engineers.

Both the development and test teams have brainstorming sessions over these two documents. They understand requirements and software design.

In the case when a new version of the software is conceptualized (when the software release is not for any specific customer but to add new features and functionalities in the core software), the CTO (chief technology officer) decides which new features and functionalities will be added. Based on features and functionalities to be added, business analysts make an SRS document and a software architect creates a mock-up document.

5.6.5 Test Automation

Because in new versions old functionality has to be tested to make sure all of these functionalities are working in the new version as well, the number of regression test cases keep increasing. To reduce total test effort on new versions, these regression test cases must be automated.

The test team used keyword-driven and data-driven automation. Here are the typical steps for doing automation.

5.6.5.1 Steps for Test Case Automation

1. Automation for functional as well as performance regression testing is done by first verifying which test cases will be in the regression cycle in this version of the application for which testing has to be performed. This is especially true if this version is a customer-specific version, as some functionality of the application is changed for any specific customer.
2. Verify if test data exists in the test bed that has been prepared. If not, then test data has to be created. Also verify location of the test data. If test data has to be fetched from a database or from any file on the network, then the mechanism for fetching the data has to be verified and documented. If test data is not available, then test data is created and documented.
3. Test cases for which script already exists are examined by automation engineers. Modification is done if any modification is required.
4. From the test cases, steps that are same for many test cases are identified. A keyword is created and assigned to these steps. Care should be taken so that the keyword is unique and the name can be easily identified with the steps for which the keyword was created.
5. A complete suite of test cases for a module for which no script already exists is recorded using QTP for functional testing and LoadRunner for performance testing. This recording is done in two phases. In the first phase, record for the steps for which keywords have been created. Save each recorded script separately and name them the same as the keyword. In the second phase, record for all test cases.
6. In the second phase of recorded script, delete the scripts for which a keyword has been created. In these places call the script using the keyword so that these steps become available in your script.
7. In the recorded script, manually insert the checkpoints wherever required.
8. In the recorded script, manually or using features of QTP or LoadRunner change the script so that the data can be fetched from the source specified in step 2. This will make your script data driven.

This is the fastest method to use keyword-driven automation along with data-driven test automation. Your script will be maintainable and your customer will be impressed with the speed with which you achieved automation.

5.7   Automation Framework

Significant development has happened over the last 5 years in the field of automation of testing. Before 1998, when record and playback features were unavailable in commercial, off-the-shelf automation software, testing professionals used to create testing scripts manually. It was a very resource-intensive task. Often almost the same amount of effort was required to test a component as was required to develop it. By 1998 Mercury Interactive launched their record and playback testing tools. This made automating testing less effort intensive. But still there was a lot of effort required in maintaining these scripts, as any slight changes in screen or data would cause changes in the test script. The other problem with these scripts was that for each test case, there was a script generated by the tool. So the same object with test data was repeated several times in the script. Any change in the object would require changing its properties at all of these places. This approach resulted in inefficient utilization of resources.

So some new techniques started evolving after 2001. All of them required the establishment of a framework that can be utilized when script is being written. Some of them include a data-driven automation framework, a keyword-driven automation framework, a hybrid framework, a model framework, and so on. The common thread among all these frameworks is reuse and automation of testing as much as possible. Traditionally it has been established that if a test case has to be executed more than 10 times, then it makes sense to automate it, as this much effort in executing the test case manually becomes equal to the effort in automating the test case. If the test case has to run more times than this, then the test case execution effort will be much less than the automation effort and will keep on becoming less afterward. Nowadays the approach is toward automating the entire testing process from the very beginning and no manual testing is done at all.

5.8   Test Data Management

Test data preparation, maintenance, and management are among the most important activities for software test management.

5.8.1   Data Maintenance in Production Environment

In a production environment, how can you create and maintain test data? You have live data that is being used by end users, and any erroneous, duplicate, or unrelated data may wreak havoc on the production system. You are not supposed to tamper with end user data as well. So you cannot use end user data for testing production environments. So how you are going to keep testing production environments?

Well, you can manage and maintain test data in your production environments by creating a complete set of test data that can be easily identified from regular test data. For example, you can create all your test data with a prefix QA for your string data type (which is the most common data type for master data). You can also use any other prefix or suffix with your test data, and you can have a service level agreement with your customer regarding creating and maintaining test data. Especially when you run your automated test scripts, you should be sure that they are running against the data specifically created for them and the data has not been tampered with or deleted. Maintaining test data is a burdensome task. To reduce your efforts in maintaining test data, you should make sure that test data does not get changed often. Data is changed only when absolutely required. In test cases where you need to delete old data and always create fresh data, the script should be made in such a way that it looks for old data and then deletes it before inserting new data. Periodic deletion of test data is required when test scripts create a large amount of test data. This can affect the performance of the production environment. In such cases, you should have deletion facility in the script itself so that at no time will a large amount of unnecessary test data go into the production environment.

5.9 Testing without a Formal Test Plan

Any project needs a solid project plan so that it can be executed without hurdles. Software test projects are no different. So you need a good software test project plan in hand before you can proceed with execution.

A formal test plan is a document that should provide and record important information about the test project. The project plan should include the following:

- Project and quality assumptions
- Project background information
- Resources
- Schedule and timeline
- Entry and exit criteria
- Test milestones
- Kinds of tests to be performed (functional, performance, integration, compatibility, etc.)
- Use cases and/or test cases
- Skills required
- Training needs
- Risks management

For many reasons many software development projects cannot budget enough time for complete and comprehensive testing. This happens mostly on smaller projects or implementation projects where not much change is required in packaged software that is being implemented (plain vanilla implementations). This also happens when a quick, small new version has to be introduced in the market. In such cases, test managers are left with managing the show without proper planning. How should you deal with such a situation?

Here is help!

We are providing a way to deal with such situations. Of course, it is not all roses on the way, and this help should not be used where detailed planning is a must for the project.

We can quickly go through the SRS document first to identify high-level functions of the project. Write them down. Once this is done, identify the other functions.

The strategy for test cases should be to find out negative, positive, and boundary value analysis for all test cases. One factor that helps in faster testing is to find out common mistakes that users make while using any application. For example, people make silly mistakes when they do not follow instructions written about filling input boxes. For password fields, some instructions are given such as "The field should contain at least six characters and should contain at least one numeric value." So check these conditions in the application and make test cases for these conditions.

You should also make priorities for test cases. From communication with a customer, you must have an idea about which areas of testing are critical for the customer. Prioritize these test areas and test them ahead of other areas.

5.9.1   The Drawbacks

Due to necessity you are sometimes forced to do testing without a proper plan. If the testing is for a new version of the application and if your team has been working on this application for some time, then testing without a plan is not a big issue. It happens in such scenarios, and it is not a big deal. In these scenarios, everybody on the team is familiar with the application and many people on your team may have developed competency for specific modules or specific types of testing. So it is absolutely normal to have this scenario and nobody complains much.

But if the application is new for the team, then definitely this approach has certain limitations. Some of these limitations include the following:

- Incomplete functional coverage—This kind of testing can never cover good functional aspects of the application.
- No risk management—Definitely without proper planning, risks cannot be ascertained, measured, or managed.
- Difficulty in reproducing defects.

5.10   Software Test Plan Checklist

5.10.1   Test Plan Checklist—Analysis and Review

- Is there evidence that the work product was reviewed by all stakeholders?
- Have acceptance criteria been established for the work product?
- Does the work product have a clearly defined purpose and scope?
- Are references to policies, directives, procedures, standards, and terminology provided?
- Does the work product identify any and all constraints/limitations?

5.10.2   Test Plan Checklist—Testing Activities

- Does the software test plan address information for test levels, test types (e.g., unit testing, software integration testing, systems integration testing, end-to-end testing, acceptance testing, regression testing), test classes, general test conditions, test progression, data recording, reduction, and analysis?
- Does the software test plan address test coverage (breadth and depth) or other methods for ensuring sufficiency of testing?
- Does the software test plan address planned tests, including items and their identifiers?
- Does the software test plan address test schedules and requirements traceability (or verification matrix)?
- Does the software test plan identify the environmental exposure as well as requirements for comprehensive, functional, performance, security, and compatibility testing?
- Does the software test plan provide a system overview that describes the unique complexities of the project from other similar projects?
- Does the software test plan address user guide and operations/maintenance validation?
- Does the software test plan identify any software reuse?

5.10.3   Test Plan Checklist—Test Environment

- Does the software test plan include information for test environment?
- Does the software test plan identify any test bed difference from production instance?
- Does the software test plan identify risks mitigation to ensure proper verification of the software capabilities in case there is a difference between test bed and production instance?
- Does the software test plan identify any other special test equipments required for each test bed?

■ Does the software test plan define the plans for delivering, installing, and validating the performance of each test bed? Does it also consider regression testing after test bed changes?

■ Does the software test plan include information for testing tools to be used?

5.10.4 Test Plan Checklist—Organization

■ Does the software test plan include information for the test environment?

■ Does the software test plan identify any test bed difference from production instance?

■ Does the software test plan identify risks mitigation to ensure proper verification of the software capabilities in case there is a difference between test bed and production instance?

■ Does the software test plan identify any other special test equipments required for each test bed?

■ Does the software test plan define the plans for delivering, installing, and validating the performance of each test bed? Does it also consider regression testing after test bed changes?

■ Does the software test plan include information for testing tools to be used?

5.10.5 Test Plan Checklist—Test Schedule

■ Does the software test plan depict software requirement completion milestones?

■ Does the software test plan depict software design completion milestones?

■ Does the software test plan depict software unit/integration testing completion milestones?

■ Does the software test plan depict software build completion milestones?

■ Does the software test plan depict software system testing completion milestones?

■ Does the software test plan depict software acceptance testing completion milestones?

■ Does the software test plan depict software deployment testing completion milestones?

■ Does the software test plan include a test schedule that depicts baseline?

■ Does the software test plan include a test schedule that depicts earned value management?

5.10.6 Test Plan Checklist—Test Tools

■ Does the software test plan address process control tools?

■ Does the software test plan address test automated execution tools?

■ Does the software test plan address test management tools?

■ Does the software test plan address defect tracking tools?
■ Does the software test plan address test coverage tools?

5.10.7 Test Plan Checklist—Configuration Management

■ Does the software test plan explain the configuration management approach for controlling test product?
■ Does the software test plan explain the configuration management approach for controlling test equipment?
■ Does the software test plan explain the configuration management approach for centrally located tool or decentralized tool?

5.10.8 Test Plan Checklist—Test Metrics

■ Does the software test plan identify the number of faults detected in each module?
■ Does the software test plan identify the number of requirements, design, and coding faults found?
■ Does the software test plan identify the number of errors by type (e.g., logic, computational, interface, documentation)?
■ Does the software test plan identify the number of errors by cause or origin?
■ Does the software test plan identify the number of errors by severity (e.g., critical, major, cosmetic)?
■ Does the software test plan identify the number of errors by priority (e.g., showstopper, medium, low)?

5.10.9 Test Plan Checklist—Project Tracking for Unit/Integration Testing

■ Does the software test plan describe the routine test progress reporting approach?
■ Does the software test plan describe the build test verification methodology?
■ Does the software test plan describe the build environment?
■ Does the software test plan describe the roles and responsibilities?
■ Does the software test plan describe the entry/exit criteria?
■ Does the software test plan describe the general guidelines?
■ Does the software test plan describe the build test planning?
■ Does the software test plan describe the build test scenario development?
■ Does the software test plan describe the build test procedure preparation?
■ Does the software test plan describe the build test execution?
■ Does the software test plan describe the build test reporting?
■ Does the software test plan describe the build test archiving?

5.10.10   Test Plan Checklist—Project Tracking for Acceptance Testing

- Does the software test plan describe the acceptance test environment?
- Does the software test plan describe the acceptance test roles and responsibilities?
- Does the software test plan describe the acceptance test entry/exit criteria?
- Does the software test plan describe the acceptance test general guidelines?
- Does the software test plan describe the acceptance test planning?
- Does the software test plan describe the acceptance test scenario development?
- Does the software test plan describe the acceptance test procedure preparation?
- Does the software test plan describe the acceptance test execution?
- Does the software test plan describe the acceptance test reporting?
- Does the software test plan describe the acceptance test archiving?
- Does the software test plan describe the acceptance test methodology?

5.10.11   Test Plan Checklist—Project Tracking for System Testing

- Does the software test plan describe the system test environment?
- Does the software test plan describe the system test roles and responsibilities?
- Does the software test plan describe the system test entry/exit criteria?
- Does the software test plan describe the system test general guidelines?
- Does the software test plan describe the system test planning?
- Does the software test plan describe the system test scenario development?
- Does the software test plan describe the system test environment?
- Does the software test plan describe the system test procedure preparation?
- Does the software test plan describe the system test execution?
- Does the software test plan describe the system test reporting?
- Does the software test plan describe the system test archiving?
- Does the software test plan describe the system test procedure preparation?

Chapter 6

Software Testing Project Risk Management

Any project is supposed to be delivered at an agreed-upon time at agreed-upon costs and with agreed-upon product or service quality. If the project meets these objectives, then it is considered to be successful. If not, then it is supposed to be a failure.

The goal looks so simple. But there are always inherent risks involved in any project which undermine any or all of its objectives. Due to these risks, the project can be delayed, cost overruns may happen, or the delivered product or service may be of poor quality.

Software testing projects are no different when it comes to meeting these same objectives: delivery at an agreed-upon time, at agreed-upon costs, and at agreed-upon quality. There is one more dimension to software testing projects along with these goals: effectiveness of software testing! Even if the project deliverables look good but the testing team actually finds a fewer number of defects than anticipated (using software engineering defect estimation techniques), then the project team has failed in its job. So many times the team tries to find more defects irrespective of whether the defects are critical to the end users. This way of doing things only brings mediocrity to the project. It fails from the perspective of effectiveness of efforts put into the project. If the team has not found critical defects that are later found by end users, then no matter how the team defends itself they have failed miserably.

Any software product may have different kinds of defects, and their impact on the product may be different. That is why we have must-fix defects and not-so-critical defects. Effectiveness applies more to these must-fix defects. So the testing team's performance is measured in terms of how many must-fix defects have been found by them and later on, when the tested application is used by end users, how many must-fix defects are found by them. Effectiveness of the testing is known only at that time.

Some of the risks that could impact a software testing project include communication gaps, cultural risks, skills risk, experience on technology risks, process risk, project size risk, infrastructure risk, overcommitment, poor planning, and so on. As software testing project manager, you have to find ways to mitigate these risks for your project. First, you will have to identify all kinds of risks specific to your project. Then you will have to plan to mitigate these potential risks.

Each risk has its own intensity of impact on the project. The intensity of each risk should be measured so that its impact on the project can be measured. There are some methods to measure impact of risk on the project. It can be measured using heuristics and intuition or using a quantitative method like assigning weights to each risk or putting a dollar value to each risk. There is not yet any method that can quantify the exact impact of a particular risk on a project. It is because no two projects are exactly the same and the intensity of any risk will be different on these projects. So the best approach is to use a combination of these methods. For this reason the test manager must have experience in executing similar projects so that he can apply heuristics and intuition to the project risks to some extent after using other methods to evaluate and assess the impact of risks on his project. How much weight should the project manager assign to each identified risk? This is a big question, and there is no easy answer to this. Here again experience counts. For instance, if you have never worked on a software development project for a Web application for a popular portal, you will never understand the impact of a risk of unavailability of the application to users. There could be thousands of concurrent users accessing that portal, and due to massive load on the application server, the server may fail to take this load and so the portal may become unavailable to users. Similarly a retail banking application for online access to one's account poses great security risk of data theft. The test manager may never be able to assess the risk involved if he has no prior experience in testing these applications. On the other hand, if he has prior experience, then he will put appropriately more weight to these risks and subsequently will test these aspects more thoroughly than other parts of the application.

6.1   Risk Measurement Method

Project risks can be measured using a structured approach. Here is a method that can be applied in measuring the impact of any risk on the project:

1. Create a weighing scale and assign a score to each risk.
2. Count the number of times the risk occurs in the project.

6.1.1 Create a Scale and Assign a Score to Each Risk

You have with you all the requirements and the modules that will be tested in this project. You also have done your homework and have a rough idea about the risks in the project. Now you will be conducting a risk assessment review with the development team for risks related to design and build. During the session a risk assessment questionnaire is used to structure the process. Each question is asked of the group and a consensus is reached as to the perceived level of risk. The questions are closed-ended questions with the possible responses of *low* (one point), *medium* (2 points), *high* (3 points), and *not applicable* (0 points). You can use this kind of scale, or you can devise your own scale for the job. The weighted scores can be used to identify error-prone areas of the application and to compare the application with other applications.

You will do this same exercise with your testing team to assess risks and their impact on the project related to areas such as testing skills required and what skills are available, automation tools to be used and their limitations, resources required and what resources are available, and so on.

Once you have scores for each risk, assign these weights to the risks.

6.1.2 Count Number of Times the Risk Occurs in the Project

Apart from the weight any risk has —which signifies how much impact the risk has—the impact of the risk on the project is also felt by the number of occurrences of the risk in the project. Suppose a risk has a score of 3 (high) but occurs just one time, whereas another risk has a score of 2 (medium) and occurs three times; then the first risk has a total score of 3 and the second risk has a score of 6. Thus the second risk has more impact on the project, and so the test team has to work more on this risk to mitigate it.

6.1.3 Risk Analysis Case Study

A risk assessment session was arranged for a project. Risk assessment was used to conduct a 1-hour assessment of the project's risk factors. The risk assessment session was conducted with two people from the test team and four people from the development team.

The raw data was placed in an Excel worksheet, and weighted scores were calculated for each question in each of the test documents. The data was analyzed using Pareto analysis to determine the number of questions to consider (i.e., the top 20% in terms of risk). The data was displayed on charts. The results revealed three major areas of risk. The first was the lack of user documentation about the process being automated. The second was the large number of interfaces to other systems. The third was the use of new technology (Ajax components) used in some parts of the system.

Use risk analysis to determine where testing should be focused. Because it is rarely possible to test every possible aspect of an application, every possible combination of events, every dependency, or everything that could go wrong, risk analysis is appropriate to most software development projects. This requires judgment skills, common sense, and experience. Considerations can include the following:

- Which functionality is most important to the project's intended purpose?
- Which functionality is most visible to the user?
- Which functionality has the largest security impact?
- Which functionality has the largest financial impact on users?
- Which aspects of the application are most important to the end users?
- Which aspects of the application can be tested early in the development cycle?
- Which parts of the code are most complex, and thus most subject to errors?
- Which parts of the application were developed in rush or panic mode?
- Which aspects of similar/related previous projects caused problems?
- Which aspects of similar/related previous projects had large maintenance expenses?
- Which parts of the requirements and design are unclear or poorly thought-out?
- What do the developers think are the highest-risk aspects of the application?
- What kinds of problems would cause the worst publicity?
- What kinds of problems would cause the most customer service complaints?
- What kinds of tests could easily cover multiple functionalities?
- Which tests will have the best high-risk-coverage-to-time-required ratio?

6.2 Risks Related to the Application Being Tested

- Complex—Anything disproportionately large, intricate, or convoluted
- New—Anything that has no history in the product
- Changed—Anything that has been tampered with or "improved"
- Upstream dependency—Anything whose failure will cause cascading failure in the rest of the system
- Downstream dependency—Anything that is especially sensitive to failures in the rest of the system
- Critical—Anything whose failure could cause substantial damage
- Precise—Anything that must meet its requirements exactly
- Popular—Anything that will be used a lot
- Strategic—Anything that has special importance to your business, such as a feature that sets you apart from the competition
- Third-party—Anything used in the product but developed outside the project
- Distributed—Anything spread out in time or space, yet whose elements must work together
- Defective—Anything known to have a lot of problems
- Recent failure—Anything with a recent history of failure

6.3   Kinds of Risks

Most aspects of your project pose risk for the project. If you have a shortage of resources, then you have a risk. If skills required for the project are not available, then you have a risk. If too many changes are being requested, then it poses risk. If there is a misunderstanding within the team or with a customer or subcontractor, then it is a big risk for the project. You name it and you have risk out there!

Let us see some common risks that every project faces.

6.3.1   *Communication Risks*

Communication risks pose the biggest risks on any project. They have an adverse impact when the project is outsourced. They have a severe impact when the project is offshored!

It cannot be emphasized more than if we say that 60% of the success of the project depends on good communication. If requirements and change requests for requirements are well understood, then the design of the software application will be good. This will lead to good coding. The standards like CMMI and ISO have always placed more emphasis on communication than on any other aspect of projects. Poor quality often results from poor communication.

In essence, poor communication is the single biggest risk on any project. When it comes to test projects, the test team must have good access to requirements and design documents as well as access to coding documents. If most of the communication on the project happens to be verbal and no written documents are being prepared or being followed, then it will be difficult for the entire test team to perform well in their respective assignments. Written communication must be applied for all test activities.

6.3.2   *Effectiveness*

In the initial assessment many people are happy only with the volume of defects reported. In reality, however, the effectiveness of the test team is determined by the number of must-fix defects reported. Trivial or cosmetic defects do not impact any software application. But critical and must-fix defects do.

The test manager must ensure that the test engineers understand the implications of less-than-expected effectiveness of the test team. When users start logging critical defects after deployment, the test manager should be prepared to answer for less-than-effective testing done by his team. Ineffective testing costs a lot of money to the software vendor. Unfixed critical defects that are to be fixed after deployment not only cost big money but also dent the confidence of users of the software application, and this in turn results in the poor image of the software vendor.

6.3.3 Cultural Risks

With outsourced test projects, where the majority of the team is located at offshore locations, communication and cultural risks pose the biggest threats to the project. With more and more software testing being offshored to lower-cost countries in Asia and eastern Europe, cultural issues play a major risk factor, as different cultures have different working environments, different values, different expectations, and different productivity.

6.3.4 Process Risks

Suppose a project is being executed by a company whose employees have experience working on similar projects but have not adopted any formal process methodology for executing those projects. Consider now that the same project is taken over by a company whose employees have mature processes and apply sophisticated processes in executing their projects. Do you think schedule, costs, quality, and effectiveness of testing will be the same? No! There will be a vast difference. In fact, nowadays some outsourcing service providers have devised elaborate, well-defined processes for testing different kinds of applications. These specialized services provide good value for the projects.

6.3.5 Size

The bigger the project, the bigger the risk, as complexity increases manifold compared to an increase in size. This leads to a higher rate increase in defects compared to an increase in size. At the same time, tasks required to manage development and testing of larger projects increase at a proportionally higher rate. As one gains experience from working on larger projects, one learns about managing them.

6.4 Challenges

Understanding software defects, finding defects, and reporting them does not ensure that the software quality has improved. Fixing those defects indeed improves software quality.

To mitigate damages caused by risks, you first need to evaluate risks correctly and the impact they may have on your project. Once this is done, you can then think of trade-offs. For example, hiring a less experienced software test engineer is a risk too.

In outsourced projects, the biggest risk factor from the customer's perspective is quality because most of the engagements are on a time and material basis. On projects that are of fixed cost–fixed time type, the biggest risk factor is cost or time overrun. So type and impact of risks also depend on the type of outsourcing contract.

Evaluating risks correctly and trading off risks with cost factors should be employed to determine whether mitigating any particular risk is cost-effective. It is impossible to mitigate all risks. So in cases when mitigating risks is not cost-effective, a trade-off may work. For instance, detecting and fixing all critical defects is impossible in a limited time frame. So a time limit must be applied for defect detection and defect fixing. Within this time limit, if some defects could not be caught, then they should be allowed to go into production. A solution for a work-around for them can be devised. This will be more cost-effective.

6.5   Checklist for Risk Management

- Does the software test risk plan address schedule estimation risk?
- Does the software test risk plan address resource estimation risk?
- Does the software test risk plan address budget estimation risk?
- Does the software test risk plan address communication risks?
- Does the software test risk plan address effectiveness risk?
- Does the software test risk plan address cultural risks?
- Does the software test risk plan address process risk?
- Does the software test risk plan address size risk?
- Does the software test risk plan address technological risks?
- Does the software test risk plan address shortage-of-skill risk?

Chapter 7

Software Testing Project Execution

In an ideal world, project planning would be the main task and project execution would be like pressing a button to start and finish it. Alas, this is not the case. In many industries execution is still the king. It is because despite all the advances in automation and standardization of process, executing any plan is still difficult. The road to execution is laden with unimaginable pitfalls and unavoidable circumstances which ensure that execution is a challenge and not a walk in the park.

Imagine you have made a good project plan, you have a good set of people in hand, you have good experience in handling testing projects, you have a good reputation with your customer, you are dedicated to the task, and you are determined to excel in the task.

So you think you have a good test project plan with most of the risks covered, good effort estimation done, and project strategies well defined. Well, only 5% of your job is done. Now you should be ready for the remaining 95% of the job. And this part of the job is more challenging, because you will face real problems, issues, challenging situations, and conflicts that will require your tact, patience, ability to make fast decisions in stressful situations, good reporting, and many more qualities.

If you are working on an iterative and incremental development model such as product development, then you will need to spend more time in understanding the architectural and functional model of the application as well as development framework so that for new releases you will be able to plan for testing without the need to have elaborate requirements and specifications for the new release (which are scarce commodities in such environments). So if you are new to this environment, then you should try to get as much information on these topics as possible by going through product documentation, attending knowledge transfer sessions, going through the application by login with different roles in the application, and finding out about process flow, workflow, business logic, and so on. Once you are comfortable with the application, it will become easier for you to test it and make plans to test it.

For outsourced projects, it is very important that along the execution cycle you provide status reports from time to time. For this reason it is extremely useful to track your project using earned value management (EVM).

7.1 Earned Value Management

Whenever a project is initiated, there is a value associated with it against the costs that will be incurred in executing that project.

There is a big difficulty in implementing EVM in software projects. The reason is that in software projects, it is very difficult to make good estimates for efforts. That is why most software projects are executed on a time-and-material basis instead of on a fixed cost–fixed schedule basis. In such a scenario, using complex metrics like EVM is even more difficult (see Figure 7.1).

However, in software test projects, it is still possible. Software projects that are offshored and where the service provider has many projects going on at any time are especially amenable to EVM implementation. This is because, due to extensive project execution knowledge, the service providers have a good repository of knowledge on which they can depend for new projects. The repository can provide critical information on which new projects can be estimated to a great accuracy. So EVM can definitely be applied for offshored software test projects (see Figures 7.2 to 7.4).

Now let us consider how we can implement EVM in software test projects.

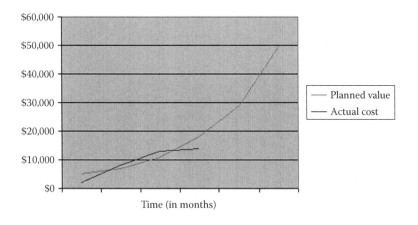

Figure 7.1 Project tracking without earned value.

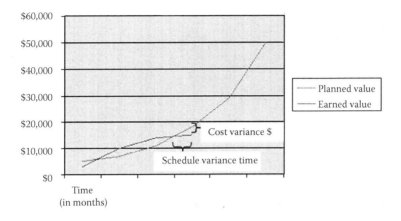

Figure 7.2   Schedule variance in project execution (variance by time and cost).

7.1.1   Need for EVM

Any project is initiated to create value for the organization for which the project was conceived. If for some reason, at any stage of the project, things get delayed or resources are wasted, then it puts a question mark on the promised delivery of the project. If you track a project just in terms of percentage of work completed or percentage of budget spent, then it is difficult to know if the project is on track or ahead of schedule or is lagging behind. From this information it is also not clear as to what factors are causing delays or wasting of resources.

For this very reason, it is important to keep a clear charter of the project and its progress at any given time to know where the project is heading. By charting an ideal course of progress for the project from the start and comparing it with actual progress of the project, you can clearly see what factors, if any, are causing problems

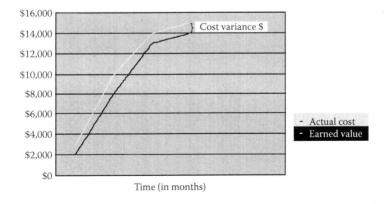

Figure 7.3   Cost variance in project execution.

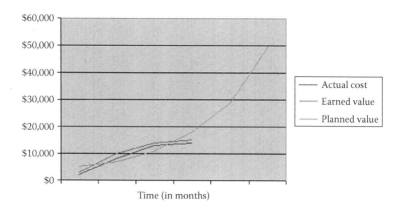

Figure 7.4 Complete earned value chart for the project depicting actual cost, earned value, and planned value.

in the project and what appropriate actions can be taken to remedy this situation. For instance, using EVM, it is possible to know which task in the project is getting delayed and what impact it can have on the entire project as well as on other tasks in the project. At the same time it will also give information as to how much impact it can have on the project.

EVM is also extremely useful in providing status reports to stakeholders of the project. It provides information such as when the project will finish given the current status, how much it will cost to finish the project, how the project performance fares against similar projects, how much it is costing to earn each unit of forecasted value, and so on.

EVM has good capability for reporting at program and portfolio levels. With many software service providers executing a lot of projects simultaneously, this becomes a handy tool to make reports at the program level for individual customers (having many projects being outsourced to the service provider) and make reports at the portfolio level for projects being executed at the departmental level.

7.1.2   EVM Implementation for Software Projects

Some of the assumptions that are needed before we move on to discussing implementing EVM for software test projects are as follows:

1. The project is not on a time-and-material basis: If this is the case, then required information necessary for calculating earned values will not be available for the project.
2. The project has relevant values available for baseline and actual information at any given time when a status report has to be made.

The primary requirement for implementing EVM is that you create a baseline schedule, budget, and resource requirement for your project. That means, at the very outset, you have complete information for your project including budget, schedule, and resource requirement. From this information you create baseline information for your project. From the baseline information you create an ideal progress path for the project. As the project progresses, you track your project by comparing actual values for cost and schedule to the baseline values.

To adopt the EVM methodology for software projects, certain modifications in the way software projects are tracked need to be made. One such requirement is that a gate should be introduced in the project before completion of any phase. The project will not progress to the next phase unless the quality standards are met for that phase. To track projects at the portfolio or program level, a standard framework for stages and gates that will apply to all projects should also be implemented. The determination of the relative cost for completing a stage based on industry standards or past project performance should be made available. The definition of the work breakdown structure, outlining the work products/deliverables to be produced at each stage/phase of the project, should also be made available. The projects should have the capability to calculate total effort associated with producing each work product. The standard rate per hour for each project should be defined to avoid disclosing the salaries/costs associated with the team members. The number of resources assigned to each work product, which together with the estimated effort and standard cost determines the total cost for each work product, should be defined. A procedure to capture actual effort and costs associated with each work product should be defined in order to report deviations from the scheduled earned value determined by the model.

If these changes can be introduced in software project processes, then EVM can be implemented successfully.

7.1.3 Audit Trail

Nowadays government regulations compliance has become an important part of most activities performed by any business house. The Sarbanes–Oxley Act (Public Company Accounting Reform and Investor Protection Act of 2002) provides provision for information to be made available to government agencies. To comply with this act, software applications now include audit trail functionality so that any financial or accounting transactions can be tracked to know if any modifications were made in that transaction in the past.

For complying with the audit trail, EVM becomes a useful tool because in EVM the baseline and actual project information is kept and can be shared at any time.

7.2 Defect Tracking and Life Cycle

Once test cases start getting executed, the test team starts finding defects in the system. They have to report these defects in the proper manner so that the defects can be tracked, fixed, and closed after verification.

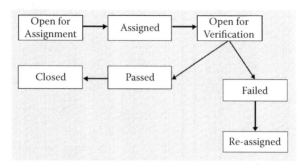

Figure 7.5 Defect life cycle.

The life cycle of a defect includes open for assignment, assigned, open for verification, failed, reassigned, passed, or closed (see Figure 7.5).

In the defect tracking system, the tester should open a new defect when he finds it. He should use a proper template for defect logging so that it will be easier for everybody in the loop who is responsible for assigning defects, fixing defects, reassigning defects, and closing defects.

Here is a template that can be used for reporting defects:

Name of tester:
Version or build: <Version or build of the product>
Module or component: <mention here the name of tested module or component>
Platform/operating system:
Type of error: <coding error/design error/suggestion/UI/documentation/text error/
    hardware error >
Priority:
Severity:
Status:
Assigned to:
Defect name:
Test data:
Steps to create defect:
Expected result:
Actual result:

7.3   Monitoring of Production Systems

Most of the production instances are tested nightly to check if the application is available or not available, if any functionality of the application has any problems, or if the application has any performance issues.

Table 7.1   Structure of a Test Case Execution Sheet

Test Case No.	Date Created	Module	Steps to Reproduce	Expected Result	Actual Result	Execution Result (Pass/Fail)	Comments

There are some issues involved in monitoring production instances. To run sanity tests, you need to have some testing data in the production instance database. These data have three issues. First, this test data should be completely isolated from production data that is critical to the business. This test data should never interfere with production data. Second, the test data should be such that it should not get deleted by any DBA or anybody responsible for maintaining the database. Otherwise the test scripts cannot run. The best convention is that you should use some prefix or suffix with this data to identify that it is for testing purposes only. For instance, you can add a prefix like "qa_" with each test data. Third, the test scripts should never generate too much transaction data. Otherwise the database will be cluttered with unwanted data. So test scripts should be written such that if any transaction data is created, then the script should delete that data after the testing run is over.

The nightly sanity tests should be completely automated so that they can be executed fast, and no test engineer should do it manually. It should run automatically at a specified time so that no human intervention is needed to start them.

Whenever a patch is applied on the production instance, the sanity test suite must be run to ensure that all application functionality is working fine.

7.4   Test Case Execution

One bottleneck during test execution is that many test cases may be dependent on each other. If the first test case fails, then the dependent test case will also fail. If the first test case has failed, then there is no point in executing the second test case. In software testing parlance this is called the showstopper defect. Unless the first test case passes, the dependent test cases cannot be executed. So apart from the usual categories of defects—that is, minor, medium, and severe defects—we have an additional category called showstopper. The development team must fix this defect as a priority so that test case execution does not get affected badly (see Table 7.1).

7.5   Checklist for Test Execution

- Has test data been created and validated?
- Has an inventory of test cases been created?
- Have regression test cases been identified and created for this release of the application?

- Have logical groups of similar test cases been created?
- Have test cases and test data been reviewed and approved by customer?
- Are all test support resources available?
- Have expected results of each test case been defined?
- Have automation scripts for all automated test cases been completed?
- How do actual results compare with expected results for all test cases?
- Have detected defects been fixed and verified? If not, is a work-around provided?
- Has the final unfixed defect list after execution cycle completion been provided?

Chapter 8

Software Testing Project Reporting

The main tasks in software test management are review of requirement and design documents, issue resolution related to these documents, risk analysis, resource planning, configuration management, test bed requirements and preparation, test project planning, test case design, test case construction, test execution, defect tracking, defect density, defect fixing verification, test entry criteria, and test exit criteria.

Of all these reports, the most important reports are the ones related to defect reporting, defect tracking, and defect fix verification. This is because the test team is paid for verifying the software application and making sure that the application is as defect-free as possible. So during test execution they report any defects found and again verify whether the defect has been fixed properly.

From statistical methods it is possible to determine the approximate number of defects in an application. Initially when test execution starts there will be a greater number of defects detected. Over time, the rate of defect detection will decline. It is possible to find how many undetected defects are still remaining in the application at any given time during the test execution phase. So it is possible to determine when to stop running test execution if a certain trade-off is to be achieved among time, resource utilization, and acceptable level of defects remaining in the system.

It also makes sense to know that software testing is not only about finding and fixing defects but also about knowing how many defects there are in the application, how many of them are must-fix defects, how many bugs have been detected by the test team in a specific period of time Project reporting helps to find out about these defects.

8.1 Importance of Reporting

You are a hardworking guy and you do your work honestly. You have done brilliantly on your project and achieved all milestones in record time. But you also happen to be a poor communicator. So when it came time to report your success story, you did your job poorly. All your status reports were also not reported properly. So even though you and your team worked hard and did the job splendidly, your customer is not happy, as he feels that the job was not done properly.

Why is this so? It is because reporting is as crucial as performing on your tasks. It is extremely important that your report have appropriate information, and it should be presented in a very clear and concise manner.

8.1.1　What Should Go in a Report

Any customer wants to see value in any project. Value comes from a better return on any customer's expenses compared to returns from similar projects. The main elements of any reports are meaningful measurements, comparison information, and good presentation. These are the three pillars of any report.

8.1.2　Case Study

Let us look at a case study from a different field to understand the importance and power of reporting.

I had moved recently to a new rented apartment. The electricity bill used to come every 2 months. From the apartment owner and some neighbors, I learned that the electricity bill came to about $80 for every 2 months if you do not operate air conditioners in your apartment. The first bill was around $79. So I thought I was fine. Actually I am very concerned about expenses, and I want to be doubly reassured that all my expenses are within reasonable limits. I became concerned when my next electricity bill was a whopping $400. I phoned the call center of the electricity distribution company and explained my situation. I also told them that in the last six 2-monthly reports (it was also printed on the bill), the bill never exceeded $90. I also explained that the bill should have been on the lower side, as my electricity consumption should have been less because it was winter and in the winter I stop using ceiling fans and window coolers. I also do not use a water heater. In effect, in winter I use electricity only for lighting and running some gadgets like the television, computer, and refrigerator. The call center executive checked my records and then told me to check the earthing (earthing or grounding is a mechanism to prevent accessible parts from acquiring a dangerous voltage in the event of a failure of electrical insulation). There is an indicator bulb provided on the electricity meter, and if it is glowing, then I have an earthing problem. Due to faulty earthing, electricity is passing and getting consumed through the circuit even when no electricity is being consumed purposely. I checked the earthing indicator and found that it was glowing. This meant that I had an earthing problem. The call center executive also told me that it is the consumer's responsibility to get it fixed and that the electricity distribution company does not have any responsibility in such cases. I immediately checked with a local electrician and made an appointment. He came and checked my electricity connections. He found that the earthing was indeed faulty. He suggested removal of earthing wires from places in the house wherever they were faulty. So he removed those wires. After that the earthing problem was solved. Now the indicator was not glowing.

I was now very much satisfied.

Let us analyze the whole episode. Why did I immediately get provoked when I received the bill of $400? It is because I had solid information that the bill should be $80 or below. When it came in at $400, I had a reason to be concerned. This knowledge came from information from previous bills. The call center executive could pinpoint the cause of the problem from seeing my previous bills and also common problems that had happened to other consumers in the area.

Even though this case study is not related to software testing at all, it shows the importance of reports. From even a simple report, you can research any problem area related to the report and get it fixed.

8.2   Test Report

The test report is the primary work deliverable from the testing execution phase (Figure 8.1). It disseminates the information from the test execution phase that is needed for project managers, as well as the stakeholders, to make further

Test summary identifier
Objective
Summary

Variances
    1. Effort Variance
    2. Schedule Variance

Activity
Defects
    1. Test defect by test phase
    2. Test defect by severity level
    3. Accepted vs. rejected test defects
    4. Defect density

Efficiency
    1. Test Execution Efficiency
    2. Test Review Efficiency

Figure 8.1   Test execution cycle report template.

decisions. Anomalies and the final decomposition of the anomalies are recorded in this report to ensure that the readers know the quality status of the product under test.

8.2.1 Test Report Components

What information should go in a report? As mentioned in the section "Importance of Reporting," any report should have information about measurements and comparison and should be presented in a concise and clear manner.

In a test report, variances for schedule and effort must be mentioned. Better yet, if you can keep EVM information, then information about budget at completion (BAC), cost performance indicator (CPI), and schedule performance indicator (SPI) should be good in all your status reports.

Next comes information about test execution information. Here you should include defect density, number of defects, number of fixed defects, defects by severity level, and so on.

Next comes efficiency data. Here you can mention test creation productivity, script creation productivity, and test execution efficiency.

8.2.1.1   Acceptance Criteria

In the user acceptance testing (UAT) report, you must include the acceptance criteria details. The UAT report must conform to acceptance criteria. So it is very important that you understand all points mentioned in the acceptance criteria document and prepare for your UAT testing accordingly.

8.2.1.2   Accessibility Testing

Your report should reveal whether accessibility testing is part of your project or not. If it is, then include an accessibility testing report in your reporting.

8.2.1.3   Status Report

At the end of each phase, you must prepare a project performance report to be sent to customers and project stakeholders. In this report, include reports for costs, schedule progress, problems encountered, delayed and on-time tasks completion, and so on.

8.2.1.4   Blocked Test Cases

The test report should contain information about all blocked test cases. These test cases have been blocked because they lack certain preconditions for executing them. For example, the UI has not been made, a showstopper test case has not been fixed upon which the test case in question cannot be executed, and so on.

8.2.1.5   Boundary Value Coverage

How many test cases have been tested with boundary values in your project? The test report should include information for the number of test cases and the number of test case where boundary value has been checked.

8.2.1.6   Test Charter

The test manager should include test charter in his test report, providing details like objective of tests, major benefits, major tasks to be performed, and so on. Good test charters help in creating a stimulating atmosphere for the team and stakeholders of the project to achieve better results out of the whole effort put into the project.

8.2.1.7   Test Bed

The test report should contain specifications for the test beds that were used for testing purposes. Test bed information should also contain information as to how it will be different from the actual production environment if the test bed is meant to perform UAT tests.

8.2.1.8   Test Basis

The test report should contain information about the documents that were used to create test cases, test case designs, test scenarios creation, test data preparation, test bed preparation, and so on. Test basis is important because it provides information such as why test coverage does not include certain application components or why certain kinds of testing were not performed.

8.2.1.9   Test Approach

Basically it is test execution approach that is covered under the test approach document. Based on the information available to the test team, it describes why a certain approach for testing was chosen and what kind of results can be expected after execution of testing.

8.3   Test Metrics

No discussion of software test reporting will be complete unless we discuss the test metrics.

When you are analyzing and measuring results of a test execution cycle, you have a lot of data. What does all this data mean to you or the stakeholders of the project? It is important to know how you are measuring, but it is equally important to know first what you are measuring and in what context. Cem Kaner [1] has discussed this subject in depth. We have ample examples in our lives to this end. Measuring anything without context is of no use.

Consider this test metric. We have effort variation, which measures actual testing effort against planned estimated effort (in man-months). Schedule variation is measured as actual testing duration compared to planned duration. We have defect density, which is measured in defects found per hour during the test execution cycle. Productivity during test case creation is measured in terms of the number of test cases created per hour. Productivity during test case execution is measured in terms of the number of test cases executed per hour. Load factor is measured as to how heavily the test team is loaded (working hours are assumed to be 8 hours per working day). Review efficiency is measured in terms of the number of defects detected per hour. Testing efficiency is measured in terms of the total number of defects detected by the testing team compared to the total number of defects detected by end users after the application goes into production.

But again no measurement is complete unless you also specify the context in which the measurement was done.

In our case, some of the context could be the following:

1. Experience of test engineers
2. Qualification of test engineers
3. Size of application under test (remember, complexity and number of defects increase exponentially more compared to increase in application size)
4. Application design complexity
5. Application design robustness (better design → fewer defects in the application)
6. Clarity in requirements (less clear requirements → more defects)
7. Coding standards (better coding standards → fewer defects)

All of these contexts themselves are subjective. In a nutshell, it is impossible to get objective test metrics and we can never achieve 100% absolutely objective test metrics. So, when you create your metrics, be sure to provide the context. Otherwise the metrics will be meaningless.

8.3.1 Metrics and Reports

Then there is the story of the village lad who cried wolf when none existed just to play a prank on his mates. But when a real wolf came along, nobody came to his rescue, as they thought he was again playing a prank on them. But this time the wolf ate his sheep. This applies to your project reporting as well. Never give false reports about your project. Otherwise, when you really are in danger, nobody will listen to you. Shout only when you need to. It is also important that when you need help, you must shout loud and clear so that it can be heard properly by those who matter.

So when you have solid metrics in your hand and you see problems, do not delay in sending the report (Figure 8.2 and Figure 8.3). Reports with solid metrics will always be welcomed.

Project	Effort Variation	Schedule Variation	Defect Density (Defects/Hour)	Productivity (TC Creation) TCPs/Hours	Productivity (TC Execution) TCPs/Hours	Load Factor	Review Efficiency	Testing Efficiency

Figure 8.2   Elements of test metrics.

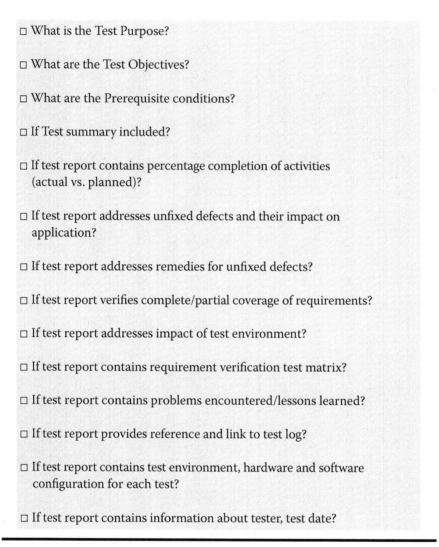

☐ What is the Test Purpose?

☐ What are the Test Objectives?

☐ What are the Prerequisite conditions?

☐ If Test summary included?

☐ If test report contains percentage completion of activities (actual vs. planned)?

☐ If test report addresses unfixed defects and their impact on application?

☐ If test report addresses remedies for unfixed defects?

☐ If test report verifies complete/partial coverage of requirements?

☐ If test report addresses impact of test environment?

☐ If test report contains requirement verification test matrix?

☐ If test report contains problems encountered/lessons learned?

☐ If test report provides reference and link to test log?

☐ If test report contains test environment, hardware and software configuration for each test?

☐ If test report contains information about tester, test date?

Figure 8.3　Checklist for a software test project report.

Bibliography

1. Kaner, Cem. 2004. "Software Engineering Metrics: What Do They Measure and How Do We Know?" Presentation, 10th International Software Metrics Symposium, Metrics 2004.

Chapter 9

Automated Software Testing Benefits

Software testing constitutes more than 50% of all effort required in any software development project. Starting from unit and integration testing to black box testing (functional and performance testing), the software goes through rigorous testing at all phases of software development until it is deployed and used by customers. Even after all this testing, end users find defects in the software, and either these defects are then fixed or some acceptable work-around is provided in the production instance.

Due to the labor-intensive nature of software testing, efforts have been made to automate some or all of the processes by many software vendors who specialize in developing testing tools. These automation efforts have been particularly beneficial in regression testing, as the same test cases are executed in almost all releases of any software. Manually executing these regression tests again and again is costly. Another aspect is that over a period of time you end up with a growing pile of regression tests to be performed in each release of the software and yet you have only a limited pool of resources to run these tests. If these test cases are automated, then a lot of manual effort can be saved. This also results in avoiding human error and monotonous work for people who have to execute the same test cases again and again. This scenario is also true for nonfunctional test automation (e.g., performance testing, load testing, stress testing). Benefits include fast execution of test cases, fast building of test cases, avoidance of human error, etc.

Test automation is also beneficial in the production environment. In the production environment, sanity tests are run daily to check critical functionality and performance bottlenecks so that if any problems are found, they are fixed immediately. Similarly, whenever any patch has to be applied in any production environment, the patch is tested in a test environment using sanity tests. If sanity tests pass in the test environment, then the patch is applied on the production environment. These sanity and performance test cases are also good candidates for automation.

Coupled with offshoring, automated testing provides a compelling business impact. It can reduce the overall cost of testing by more than 70% over a mid-range to long period of time. The offshoring partners create a central test organization and utilize shared resources, methodology, and knowledge repository across all of their customer engagements to provide consistent, superior, fast, and very cost-effective ways to provide better results for you. For this exercise they create centers of excellence at their development centers so that they have a pool of test architects, automation engineers, functional consultants, and test leads. Whenever any project comes, a team is formed and depending on workload across all projects, these resources are allocated to the project depending on availability. This approach provides not only a means of better utilization of resources (skilled resources are never sitting idle on the bench for want of project work) but also consistency and superior testing effort and results.

Some of the often-cited benefits of test automation include the following:

- People lose interest in manually executing the same test cases (regression tests) repeatedly and become reluctant to do it. Automation provides a good escape from such scenarios.
- Return on investment—If the same test case has to be executed more than five times (which is often the case for most regression tests), then the cost of licensing the tool, deploying automation engineers, and using time to create the test script is justified. The ROI will depend on the cost of the automation tool license, the effort required to write test scripts, and the salary of automation engineers.
- Fast execution—If a test suite takes 3 hours to execute manually, using automation script and running it may take just 15 minutes. So you may end up saving a large amount of time in winding up your testing. This will also ensure that your new release will go to market in record time and costly delays in marketing your product can be avoided.
- Avoid manual errors—Executing test cases manually can lead to human error. Running these test cases using an automation tool will avoid these manual errors.
- Avoid need of additional resources—With the number of regression tests growing exponentially over software releases, additional resources are required to run these tests. With the introduction of automation, additional resources may not be required.

9.1   Considerations for Automation

The business world tries to automate every activity that is performed by human beings. The reasons are too many! Automation saves on labor costs, eliminates human error, increases productivity, brings information online and in real time, and so on. But not all activities can be automated.

In the case of software test management, some amount of automation has been successful in areas like test case execution, test case management, requirements management, and so on. When we talk of automation in software test management, currently we are referring to test case execution management to a large extent.

9.1.1   Analysis of Test Case Activities

All of you have been hearing a lot about software test automation and its stupendous benefits. But have you ever wondered how many of the activities involved in software testing can actually be automated?

Let us analyze the activities that are involved in a typical GUI level regression test.

1. Analyze the specification and other docs for ambiguity or other indicators of potential error.
2. Analyze the source code for errors.
3. Design test cases.
4. Create test data.
5. Run the tests the first time.
6. Evaluate the first result.
7. Report a defect from the first run.
8. Debug the tests.
9. Save the code.
10. Save the results.
11. Document the tests.
12. Build a traceability matrix (tracing test cases back to specifications or requirements).
13. Select the test cases to be run.
14. Run the tests.
15. Record the results.
16. Evaluate the results.
17. Measure the results (e.g., performance test results, functional test results).
18. Report and analyze errors.
19. Maintain, update, and debug the tests.

Of all the activities listed above, only the activities mentioned in points 14 and 15 can be automated. The rest of the activities will always depend on human testers and cannot be automated. Point 18 can be partially automated, as analyzing the results is always a human activity but error reporting can be automated fully.

9.1.2 Financial and Execution Time Impacts

Still it cannot be denied that automation of test case execution yields benefits. For a large packaged enterprise software application, a suite of regression test cases could easily run in more than several thousand test cases. Suppose that, on average, each test case requires an execution time of 2 minutes; then the total time required for running all regression test cases could be more than 4000 minutes (66 hours). That means it will take more than eight working days if one person is assigned to run these test cases manually. To reduce this execution cycle, the software vendor or his service provider partner can assign eight people to complete the regression test case execution in 1 day. Now suppose the average salary and other benefits of employees are $2000 per week. So the software vendor spends more than $2000 to run the regression test cases for release of his software application. In addition to this amount of money, the software vendor is spending more than one extra day in the release cycle. Now suppose that all test cases have been automated and it takes 10 seconds to run each test case by the automation tool. Then the time required to execute all regression test cases comes to more than 330 minutes (5 hours). In this case the software vendor not only is able to shrink the release cycle but will also save more than $2000.

Now suppose the company employs automation engineers to create automation scripts for these 2000-odd test cases. Suppose they take 15 minutes to automate each test case. That means it will take 500 hours to automate all test cases. So an automation engineer will take 63 days to complete his assignment. Again suppose the regression test suite runs once in every quarter (company releases new versions once every quarter). Over a period of 5 years, the regression test suite will run 20 times. As we have already seen, the automated execution saves 61 hours in each cycle; the time saving over the 5-year period will be 1220 hours. At the same time, effort saving in terms of money spent in salary of the manual tester for executing regression test cases for the 5 years will be $40,000. Though the money savings is not big enough, the time savings is definitely a big differentiator. Time to market is such an important factor that any time saving in a new release cycle is a big plus.

So the secret of being successful in automating does not lie with blindly automating test cases without thinking about what activities are being automated. Along with automation, you also need to think about how to make the manual activities that cannot be automated more efficient.

9.1.3 Workload Factor

Let us consider a business scenario for a software application vendor who makes large enterprise applications. In the first release of the application, it took a team of five test engineers to verify and validate the product in 10 business days. In the next

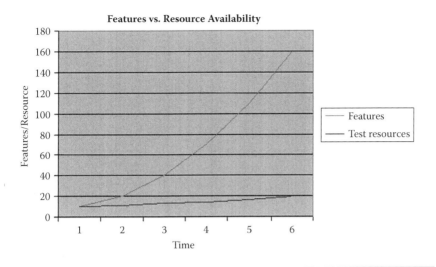

Figure 9.1   Feature increase vs. resource availability.

release (after a quarter), it took eight test engineers to verify and validate the new version of the application in 14 business days. After 5 years the scenario was like this. It took 180 test engineers to verify and validate the next quarterly release of the application in 12 business days. In all releases of the software, testing execution was done manually and no automation was used.

Question: Why did the software vendor need so many testing resources in the later release of the application? It is because over the 5-year time span, features in the application had increased 10-fold and the existing features had also been enhanced considerably. Out of the 180 test engineers deployed, 50 engineers were exclusively dedicated to regression testing. Now the regression testing suite had grown to more than 4500 test cases. Adding, maintaining, and running the suite of regression test cases manually had become a huge task.

From Figure 9.1 it can be seen that with increasing feature addition over time in an application, testing resource requirements increase; however, finding these resources is difficult.

This factor calls for automation of regression test cases.

9.2   Test Automation History

When the software industry was in its infancy (the dark mainframe era!), software testing was not a sophisticated process, as can be imagined. Almost all software testing was manual. Then, in the client server era (1970s), MIS departments started making their own small testing tools. Mostly it was in the areas of simulation and test bed creation. Some amount of database testing was also being automated. Then, in the 1990s, when the Internet started to make its presence felt, some testing tool vendors appeared on the horizon. These early tools were able to capture user screens and user activity during transactions. Most of this automation can be referred to as "record and play."

In recent history Worksoft and some other vendors have introduced some tools that capture the business logic of any application in such a way that even when there are changes in the application, the automation code also gets changed and thus runs without needing any maintenance of the script. This functionality is called code-free automation. Basically these tools store information on all captured objects during recording in a database and map this information when the test scripts are run. It is known as application mapping.

9.3   Case Studies

In recent years, test automation has created a lot of excitement among customers, and they have been looking to reap promised benefits. Of course automation brings benefits, but uninitiated people find it difficult to understand in what way and how many benefits can actually be realized.

Here are a few case studies for software test automation projects. In most of these cases, the customers had wrong notions of benefits arising from automation projects and needed a thorough explanation and convincing by the service provider.

9.3.1   Business Case 1

9.3.1.1   Wrong Customer Expectations

It was required to execute more than 600 test scripts within a span of 3 hours. It was required that the automation scripts should be easily maintainable and maintenance costs should be kept to a minimum. The scripts should be executed unattended.

9.3.1.2   Problem Statement

■ Customer expectations were not met.
■ Project was suspended due to low customer confidence.

9.3.1.3   Issues Faced

■ Lack of customer knowledge about what testing tools can do and what we can get out of using these tools.
■ Wrong customer expectation about amount of time required in automating test cases. The expectation was that using automation tools testing cycles will

be reduced by more than 70%. Customer also believed that the automation tool will generate testing data and so time required to generate test data either manually or using any other tool will be totally eliminated. Customer also had a wrong notion that the automation tool can run in any environment irrespective of platform, hardware, or operating system. Customer also had expectation that the automation tool will generate scripts that will detect all defects in the software application.

- Customer attitude—Customer was not ready to listen to suggestions.
- Test automation process—Customer was totally ignorant about the whole automation process including detailed procedures required.
- Test script maintenance effort—Customer was totally ignorant about the maintenance required in scripts.

9.3.1.4   Solution

- Customer expectation—Educate the customer about practical constraints, detailed test automation process, the real benefits of automation, which automation tools provide what kind of benefits, which tools are the best fit for the given scenario, what are limitations of the tools, provide detailed automation framework, provide ROI, provide technical expertise and latest trends in testing tools, explain what metrics will be delivered to customer based on type of data collected, what measures will be controlled and monitored.

9.3.1.5   Lessons Learned

It was a tough call to convince the customer about realities. Through continuous customer education it was possible for the team to explain what the real benefits are and exactly how these benefits can be realized. The team also educated the customer on the whole process to be followed in automation. The team kept the customer informed on all developments and updated him on regular intervals.

9.3.2   Business Case 2

9.3.2.1   Automation Strategy

To be successful every project should have a well-thought-out strategy before the project actually starts. In many test automation projects, ad hoc measures are taken instead of a strategy from the start. For instance, it is important that you select which test cases should be automated and which should not. Depending on complexity, the number of times the test case should be executed during regression, and maintenance needed over the number of expected regression cycles, it is very important to choose test cases for automation. Automating test cases that will not run many times or test cases that will need a lot of maintenance will be a waste of time and money. On many projects, the test team tries to automate all test cases, which is a totally wrong approach. Time taken in result analysis and reporting should also be considered.

In this particular project, all of the aforementioned considerations were not taken care of during automation.

9.3.2.2   Issues Faced

- Higher effort/time for maintenance—Because all test cases were selected for automation, effort for maintenance of automation scripts in subsequent releases of the software was huge.
- Lower regression test coverage—Due to high number of test case automation for certain parts of the application under test, other high-priority areas of the application were getting neglected, and this led to low test coverage of many high-priority areas.

9.3.2.3   Solution

To overcome the problems faced we first defined a complete test automation process including a keyword-driven framework and implementation strategy. We linked test automation strategy with requirements. Due to thoughtful execution, a lot of rework and scrap could be avoided. Because we adopted a keyword-driven framework, if any change was required in the script due to any change in software being tested, it could be done at only one place in the script. Thus script maintenance work was reduced by more than 70%. The scripts were also portable from one platform to another with minimal change in script. The keyword-driven framework also enabled domain experts to test the application easily. This approach enabled testers to test the application the way any end user may use the application.

9.3.2.4   Lessons Learned

- Process implementation—This project helped all team members to learn the right approach to executing any automation project.
- Implementation of requirement-driven approach through relevant test design techniques. Using a keyword-driven framework, requirements-based testing, highly maintainable and portable scripts, determining which tests to automate, and how to reduce scrap and rework were the best lessons the entire team learned from this project.

9.3.3 Business Case 3

9.3.3.1 Tool Selection

In this project we faced this problem that the tool did not work with the script that was developed with an earlier version of the automation tool. The tool vendor had changed functions in the new version from the earlier version and did not provide backward compatibility so that the script developed with the earlier version did not work with the new version that we were using.

9.3.3.2 Solution

The applications we were testing were manufacturing and production planning modules of Oracle's E-Business suite. We had received automation scripts for around 1200 test cases that were developed using Quick Test Pro version 8.0. One hundred ten person-months of effort were put into creating the scripts using QTP 8.0. We ported these scripts to QTP version 8.2. It required 75% of effort in porting the scripts to QTP version 8.2 compared to the effort required in originally creating the scripts.

9.3.3.3 Lessons Learned

The tool selection team should be formed before selecting a tool. This way, retraining of staff can be avoided. The automation team should verify the presence of backward compatibility of newer versions with old versions, a thorough study of the tool's capabilities and incapabilities, tracking of the newer version of the tool using evaluation versions, and compatibility of the tool with a configuration management tool so that script versions can be maintained easily. The team should also have access to 24/7 customer support from the tool vendor.

9.3.4 Business Case 4

In this case, a test project was offshored from a customer when the customer decided to take the project from the internal team. The service provider inducted fresh resources for the project. They were provided with rigorous training.

9.3.4.1 Problems

The recruited team members had different backgrounds and had no prior experience of working on similar projects. So the learning curve was slow. The team required an inordinate amount of time to learn business processes as well as to learn the testing tools. The script created by the team had a lot of errors, and these scripts never ran smoothly and used to stop due to some error in the script. This led to insufficient defect detection in the application under test. After a period of time the customer lost confidence in the project. This also led to loss of goodwill from the customer side.

9.3.4.2 Solution

Finally the project was handed over to another service provider. They had good experience in handling such projects. They finished the project in a satisfactory manner. This became possible because the new team employed techniques like efficient knowledge transition, had a backup plan in place, had a good resource center (known as center of excellence) for automation where expert automation engineers were available, and so on.

9.3.4.3 Lesson Learned

In offshoring projects, a proper knowledge transition process should be in place so that all deficiencies in knowledge and understanding about the project can be addressed.

9.3.5 Business Case 5

9.3.5.1 Test Estimation

This project faced the problem of underestimation of project size. The project execution was based on monthly plan and estimation. Estimation was based on the test steps in the manual test cases, which was a wrong approach. Again complexity was derived based on the number of steps in the manual test cases. Controlling factors were calculated based on experience of the estimator and not by statistically proved data. After the initial estimation no effort were made to refine it. Test data creation effort was not accounted in the estimation as well.

9.3.5.2 Issues Faced

Due to schedule underestimation, schedule overruns happened for almost all phases of the project. Due to effort underestimation, budget overrun also happened for all phases. This led to loss of customer goodwill.

9.3.5.3 Solution

The project was handed over to another team. This team used test point analysis for effort and schedule estimation. The team also made sure that size of the application, test strategy, and productivity were considered in effort estimation. They derived dynamic test points and static test points for calculations. They also considered quality and environmental factors in their calculations.

They broke down effort estimation for various tasks. They allocated 20% of effort for planning, 40% for test case design and script creation, 10% for maintenance of scripts, 10% for test case management with the test management tool, 10% for test case execution, and 10% for reporting and analysis.

9.3.5.4   Lessons Learned

Excellent effort estimation is the most crucial element in test management. Due to effort underestimation, the whole project could fail even though other aspects of the project are fine.

9.3.6   Business Case 6

9.3.6.1   Technical Issue

This automation project had the problem of difficulty in maintaining the scripts. Many third-party objects/controls in the application under test were not being recognized by the automation tool. Changes in object properties on the GUI led to the tool not recognizing them. These changes were happening with each new build and release. Due to these problems much critical functionality could not be tested. The goal of unattended test execution was also hampered, as many test cases could not be automated and so were executed manually.

9.3.6.2   Solution

The team first identified the objects that could not be recognized by the tool. Then they approached the software design and development team to resolve this issue. Once these objects were modified, the tool could recognize these objects and so the test cases involving those objects could be automated. Additional code was manually written for unattended execution so that in case of problems with the script, the test cases could be skipped and execution could proceed without any intervention.

9.3.6.3   Lessons Learned

Non-recognition of objects is a problem area that many teams come across. In those cases, the development team must change the code so that they can be recognized by the testing tool.

9.3.7 Business Case 7

9.3.7.1 New Technology

Rich browser technologies are increasing in use and so new technologies are being developed. AJAX technology allows dynamic and floating menus to be added to the browser-based applications. This project had AJAX components, which represent the latest technology, and testing these components was a challenge. The testing also required parsing XML data and validation of the component against this data.

9.3.7.2 Issues Faced

Not many automation tools available in the market can recognize these new tools. Parsing and validation of XML statements is also not possible with many of these tools.

9.3.7.3 Solution

Many tools were evaluated to determine if they can support this new technology. Vendor support at many vendors was queried. Finally the right tool that could support this technology was selected.

9.4 Keyword-Driven Automation Framework

The framework for software development started with the procedural model. Source code used to be organized inside procedures. These procedures could be called anywhere inside the software application. This used to facilitate code reuse, as the procedure could be passed with different kinds of data to generate different results using the same procedure. A limitation of the procedure-driven application framework was that it would not allow different implementations of the same procedure. This is required to eliminate the large number of procedures needed to do similar kinds of work in the code. Then came the object-oriented programming framework. Here a class, once created, could be implemented in different ways to do similar kinds of work. This reduced the need to create a large pool of classes to be created for the software application. This framework also allowed the possibility of child classes to be part of parent classes. This resulted in creating packages of classes that together could do many kinds of tasks by replacing a child inside a parent class with another child. These measures ensured that code reuse could be enhanced to the maximum extent possible. Object-oriented programming also helps in maintaining the code. If any change in definition of any class is required, then it is done in that class; the rest of the software changes automatically, as wherever that class is called, the changed class behavior reflects the output of that class to the whole application. So the need to change the code in a lot of places is eliminated.

So object-oriented programming has a made a huge impact in improving productivity of software developers in recent years.

Test cases contain many steps that are identical or similar to steps in other test cases. A limitation of the record-and-play type of automation is that these similar steps are recorded again and again during recording time. Thus, for the same steps across many test cases, separate scripts are generated even though they are the same pieces of code. Now if the application that is being tested gets changed, then you will have to make changes at all of these places.

Now suppose you devise a method so that the generated scripts do not repeat for the same pieces of code. Instead a placeholder for these pieces of code is placed and the code in fact is kept at just one place. The code gets called at these placeholders and gets executed. In such a scenario, maintaining the code base of the automation script will become very easy. Whenever any changes occur in the application under test, you just have to change the code base once at places where you are keeping the code. Now when that piece of code is called at placeholder places, this changed code gets executed. Thus maintenance effort will be significantly reduced and managing the automation script base will become a lot easier.

To achieve this goal, some approaches have been devised. The best one is known as the keyword-driven automation framework.

9.4.1 Steps for Creating Keyword Framework

There will not be any changes in the way test cases are written for manual execution for creating the keyword framework. So design and write your test cases. Find out which test cases have steps that are the same for other test cases. Make an inventory of these steps. Once these are ready, use your automation tool to record these steps. Input appropriate names for each of these scripts. These will be the functions that can be called inside the main script. After that, go back to your test cases and record for the entire test case suite. Now delete generated scripts for the steps for which you had done a separate recording. Now put a placeholder in place of deleted code (function calls). Call the appropriate function at these places. Now you are done.

The keyword framework is similar to procedural programming. So test automation has not reached the stage that object-oriented programming has reached. Still, using keyword framework, you are promoting code reuse and increasing productivity.

The approach described above is fast. Some other approaches are also available. Depending on the tool capability, amount of time in hand, and skills of the automation engineers, this process can be either refined further or made more granular to save time.

9.5 Data-Driven Automated Testing

When you run your test case, you repeat the test case with checks for boundary values, acceptable values, and unacceptable values to ensure that the software application under test is working fine for all kinds of user inputs. In data-driven automation testing, you iterate the test case by supplying different values to the same test case. The test data can be taken from a database or a data table, captured from a GUI, input manually in input boxes in the application, and so on.

Chapter 10

Customer Expectation Management

In today's world of outsourcing, customer expectation management is the most important part of your job function. Never mind that you do your assignments fine; if your customer is not happy over some issue, then you are digging your own grave.

What are the expectations of the customer? Good question! Depending on the kind of agreement your company has with the customer, they can vary. I am assuming that you are working for a software services company who outsources software development or software test projects from customers. This agreement could be for product development or software testing, or it could be for a software implementation project.

10.1   Difficult Proposition

Software projects are characterized by low success rates. Only about 20% of the projects are delivered within a specified budget and schedule [1]. Even within this category only about 10% of the projects deliver exactly as promised quality and other specifications. So 10% of these still miss on quality parameters. A whopping 80% of the software projects fail in terms of delivering late or over budget or not fulfilling promised functionality.

These failure rates are due to many reasons. Foremost is that software projects do not have detailed design specifications compared with the ones seen in construction, contract manufacturing, or for that matter any industry. Why do software projects not have detailed designs? Well, the cause is hidden in the nature of the software industry. The software industry is characterized by a fast and constantly changing business scenario. The average life of a software product is hardly 5 years. Hardware on which this software product runs has a still shorter life. Compared to this scenario, a building is built to last 50 years or more. Definitely it makes sense to have a detailed design for something that has such a long life. That is why software projects cannot afford to provide time to create detailed designs for the software to be built. The other reason is that even if we create a detailed design for a software system (spanning more than a year or so), then the software platform, software language, software architecture, and so on, will be obsolete by the time the software is built and ready for use.

In such a scenario, software testing becomes critical. Testers are under pressure to verify and validate the software system in a compressed timescale and yet they also have the pressure to push the product out of the door (obviously from the development team) even if the product is half-baked. On the other hand, the customer is also eager and constantly asking how much more time it will take to deploy the product. He is losing patience and is not willing to accept any explanations. Software test managers always face such prospects. They definitely are constantly in tough situations, and only the tenacious and smart guys survive in this part of the world.

10.2   Service Level Agreement

The service level agreement (SLA) is the single most important factor that can make or break any relationship between the customer and the service provider. Most of the customer expectations revolve around it. So from the very outset the SLA should be framed in such a manner that later on it will be easy for both the customer and the service provider to fall back on it whenever any dispute arises.

In the offshoring situation, SLAs become even more important. The environment in which offshored projects are executed is entirely different from the environment in which traditional in-house test projects used to operate. Due to distance, difference in culture and productivity, and many other bottlenecks, these projects need a mature delivery vehicle to build confidence with the customer. These service providers now consolidate software testing projects to reduce costs. In such a situation, it becomes difficult for the service provider to give due importance to each and every project. Some projects thus may suffer due to low priority assigned to them by the service provider. In consolidation mode, it also becomes difficult to stick to SLAs for projects that have a different scope or nature.

In such a situation, SLAs become the only tool in the armory of the customers.

10.3   Product Development

If you are working on a product development project for a software vendor, then you will be working on different versions of the same software over time. As a test professional, you are expected to work with a lot of regression testing. You are also expected to work on the production environment (software that is implemented and running at your customer's customer sites). Your team will be expected to run regression tests on these production sites whenever any new patch is applied. Also your team will be expected to do daily sanity checks on all of their sites. So the software test team is expected to do a lot of work with new releases and customer-specific implementations.

In short, you are expected to work in all phases of the product life cycle, be it the requirement stage, design, build, UAT, go live, or production. The customer expects that your team will be able to handle software testing work in all phases of the software product life cycle.

By its very nature, product development work is continuous and incremental. So the development projects and their associated test projects are short and frequent. The traditional waterfall model cannot be applied on these projects. Software testing for these kinds of projects needs to have a continuous process approach. In such situations the CMMI process model is the most suitable, as it allows integration of development, production, and maintenance activities. Software testing also revolves around these activities.

Due to the large number of test cases to be executed in regression cycles, it makes good sense to try to automate these test cases as much as possible. Customers will never wait for the time required to manually execute these large numbers of test cases every time a new release is due.

Sanity tests for production instances should also be automated, as they are run on a daily basis. Customers look to eliminate staff costs in running these tests as well as wanting to make sure that all features of the software are checked daily to verify that they are working. So sanity tests need to be completely automated and should run automatically at a specified time without any human intervention.

10.4   History

IT and MIS departments traditionally have taken care of the IT needs of any company. Before the dawn of ERPs and enterprise applications developed by software vendors, they used to develop, test, implement, and maintain all IT systems for their company. So all departments within their company used to be their internal customers. After consultation with any department, they would initiate a software project to develop a system for that specific department.

These systems used to be at the department level. Interdepartmental communication used to be on paper, and these departmental systems were not connected with each other. This led to the creation of silo-type systems. As it was a very inefficient method of interdepartmental communication, slowly these systems started to be connected with each other through some integration technologies.

The roles of these internal MIS and IT departments have changed completely over the last 50 years. After commercial ERPs were introduced in the 1970s, companies started to implement these ERPs instead of developing custom applications for their needs. But still a lot of their IT system requirements were not met by these early ERPs. Some applications were still being developed by these internal IT departments.

Nowadays these internal MIS and IT departments act as sourcing agencies as well as are responsible for maintaining IT systems that were implemented for their companies. Most of the applications are now procured from software vendors, and there is little scope for custom software development. So these departments have now become expert at evaluating software applications available in the market and finding best solutions for their companies. The number of services companies who provide evaluation services for these IT departments has also mushroomed. Some of these services companies also provide ready-made templates and questionnaires that can help these IT departments to evaluate software vendors and their applications and choose best-fit applications themselves.

For support functions, these IT departments engage service companies who are providing their specialized support services, though some amount of support and maintenance work is still carried out by these IT departments.

For software testing, these departments are doing software testing from the client perspective. They also outsource software testing to third-party service providers. Many times software testing is done by the implementing service provider.

To reduce costs, software vendors themselves have been outsourcing software product development and software testing to service providers. In such situations, the software vendor keeps some amount of software development, architecture development, and software testing with itself and outsources large parts of these activities to its partners. The software vendor controls activities of its service partner through elaborate service level agreements.

From the service provider's point of view, each account is crucial. So they form a dedicated team for both software development and software testing. To ensure that their work is of the highest quality, they adhere to best practices norms for all of their processes which are available to the industry. They assess their processes for the capability maturity model for software development, the test maturity model for software testing, and other such industry certifications. These service providers have developed a well-defined software development life cycle (SDLC) model and software testing life cycle (STLC) model, which help them to ensure that their clients have confidence that whatever their partners are working on is getting done with the highest quality. Excellent quality of work also ensures that customers of these software vendors have a good product implemented and they are satisfied. This helps the software vendor to have good confidence in their products by the market, and it also ensures that support costs for their product get reduced.

With the global economy slowing down, most end user organizations as well as software vendors have been forced to resort to low-cost alternatives for software development and software testing services. This has led to offshoring of software projects.

10.5 Challenges

With maturity of test management at a very high level (most software services companies will acknowledge that they have well-defined test processes and a rich body of knowledge acquired after executing thousands of projects over the years), any new project reporting becomes easier to manage and archive. However, software testing is a very creative profession including test automation efforts. And here just following the processes does not help, because sticking to process and creativity do not mix well. You need to provide room for creativity in the project. And the catch is that the creative portion of the project is tricky as far as reporting is concerned. So how do you deal with it?

For the structured part (which conforms to defined processes like standard metrics, e.g., defect density, defect fixing cycle, defect tracking), standard processes can be adopted. For the creative part (e.g., automation effort, test case preparation effort), effort estimation itself is difficult to predict. Using sophisticated techniques effort estimation can be predicted to some degree of accuracy. The best approach is to keep track of risk factors in effort estimation (in fact, keep them on the plus side) so that later on stakeholders are not in for any surprises. Remember, the biggest challenge a test team faces is meeting or exceeding customer expectations. The customer will never forgive you if, due to overconfidence or pressure from any stakeholders, you commit to a timeline that is not sustainable. So always keep a safe margin for your team when you do effort estimation. That way, you can always deliver something extra to your customer apart from your deliverables. "You should always commit less and deliver more!" This is what will keep you in good stead and in fact get you appreciation from your client and your management. On the other hand, if you agree to deliver goods in an unmanageable timeline and you fail to deliver in time, you have committed a sin that will not be forgiven by either the client or your management.

10.6 Requirement Analysis

When any project document is made, there are several revisions to it. These documents are never complete or accurate. This is especially true of the customer requirement document. If you are working for a product development project, then things are easier. Even customer-specific implementation of a project does not add or change many features in the product. The new user interface specifications are similar to the existing user interface, new components of user interfaces are similar to existing components, workflows are similar to existing workflows, transactions are similar to existing transactions, and so on. Adding or modifying these new features in an existing product thus does not require very detailed requirement information. Testing for nonfunctional requirements like performance, stress, and load testing is also easy, as previous behavior of the application is well known and new and modified features will not change the behavior of the application drastically.

But when it comes to custom software development, things are totally different. Nothing is known about functional and nonfunctional aspects of the application beforehand. During requirement gathering meetings the project team documents whatever is being said and expressed by the customer. Once the so-called requirements are gathered and documented, they are sent to the customer for approval. The customer adds, deletes, or modifies the requirements wherever they want changes in the original document. So now the requirement document is approved and the design team starts architecting the system. During any phase of the project, if the customer wants any changes, he communicates these changes through change requests. These changes impact the design and subsequent phases of the project.

Can the testing team rely on this requirements document for testing the application? What is the accuracy and completeness of this document? Has whatever was expressed by the customer during requirement gathering been completely covered in the document? Is whatever was expressed by the customer during requirement gathering accurate and complete? Experience shows that the essence of any communication cannot be captured 100%. Customers often do not know their requirements themselves completely. Many of their requirements are vague or incomplete. Putting all things together, one can confidently say that for testing the application, the tester cannot rely only on the requirement document. The tester has to look beyond the requirement document. Unfortunately one more limiting factor for the testing team is that they are engaged in the project late and do not have firsthand information about many things. This means they do not have many avenues for information and so they rely heavily on whatever documents they have.

One more aspect to be considered here is that with software applications user base crossing business boundaries, it is difficult to gather requirements for all users. Nowadays many applications are being used by your customer's customer. In such instances it is extremely difficult to gather all requirements.

10.7   Project Process Information

The customer should be informed about the processes that will be followed for the project in detail. This will help the customer to understand how each process is linked to other processes and how processes are implemented. Even if the service provider is assessed with the CMM maturity model and/or other process models, these models do not show how the processes defined in these models are actually implemented with the service provider. At any rate, these process models are actually nothing but processes and broad guidelines about the processes. It is up to the service provider as to how he implements them. We deal with legal and government regulations in our daily lives. The same federal rule may be implemented differently by the local municipal or state governments. Then the same rule may be implemented differently or not implemented at all by the local governing body. For instance, pollution control certification is required for all vehicles in India in all states and municipalities. But in New Delhi the traffic police never bother about this certificate. They never check whether any vehicle has a current pollution control certificate, though they check other certificates for validity.

10.8   Case Study: Electronics Retailer

For instance, there was a supply chain management application implemented for a global electronic goods distributor. The application consisted of EDI integration, inventory organization (retail stores, warehouses, products, manual/automatic replenishment), order management, and supplier database modules. This electronic distributor had many customers who are basically electronic goods retailers. In the scheme of things, this electronic goods distributor was the supplier and would use the EDI integration and inventory organization modules. Customers of this electronic goods distributor would use order management and inventory organization modules.

When the requirement-gathering team visited customer sites and met end users of the customer, they could get most of the requirements for the electronic goods distributor. But getting requirements from their customers was difficult. First of all, which of their customers will be using this system was not known at the time of requirement gathering. Second, getting requirements from all the customers would be difficult, as the electronic goods distributor was expecting that more than 70% of its customers will use the system (that meant more than 1000 customers). Getting requirements from such a huge number of customers was impossible.

The best approach in such cases is the incremental iteration development process. Whenever new requirements come, they can be integrated with existing requirements and the system is designed accordingly. This kind of development is possible only when an open architecture is adopted from the beginning so that new features can be added from time to time. These can be incorporated in new releases of the software.

10.9   Customer Expectation Management Strategies

10.9.1   Customer Involvement

It is a psychological fact that if you have to deliver something to somebody, then the other person will never understand the difficulties you face in delivering. Once he has agreed with you for delivery, he assumes that the delivery will be made at the promised time. If for some reason you face difficulties, then he will not cooperate and will blame you and will never try to understand your situation. He will only be looking at the SLAs and will never look beyond that. On the other hand, if you have created a good rapport with him early on and you have been communicating with him constantly, then he will definitely understand your situation; in cases when difficulties arise, he will cooperate and will sit with you and help you in solving the issues. That is why successful projects always have customers actively involved.

Establish an agreement that both the customer organization and the delivery organization have rights and obligations if the project is to be a success. Establish an agreement that both parties will respect each other's rights. Also in the SLAs make provision for ample and regular communication between the two by including compulsory meetings or other communication platforms at regular intervals.

It is very important in outsourced projects to keep seeking buy-in for every initiative taken by the service provider at all levels of the customer's organization. Lack of management involvement and support within the customer community can severely affect any project.

There are three aspects of communication: (1) to create a rapport, (2) to reduce errors due to misunderstandings, and (3) to keep track of the project with status reports from time to time. In fact, there are three mantras for success of any project: communication, communication, and communication!

10.9.2 Kickoff Meeting

Kickoff meetings help in breaking the ice and starting the project in a very positive environment. Arrange a kickoff meeting with the customer at the outset of the project to set the ground rules for the project and to position the project for success. Kickoff meetings are very useful in gauging and setting customer expectations from the very beginning of the project.

It is very important that the meeting takes place when everybody from the customer's project team is available and can give enough time for the meeting. Postpone and rearrange the meeting if anybody from the customer's project team cannot attend the meeting.

The agenda at the meeting should be to discuss scope, risks, known issues, and critical factors in the project. By the end of the meeting, customer expectations should be clear. Any agenda items that are not fully resolved should be assigned as issues and tracked to resolution using the formal issue management process.

10.9.3 Get Approval for Delivery Methodology

Each organization has some unique methodology to deliver projects. The service provider must educate the customer about the process so that the customer understands how deliveries will be made.

The best place for discussing delivery methodology is the steering committee. This is where top stakeholders from the customer side are available. Explain to them why you adopted the methodology for the project and why it is essential that the project be delivered this way. Once they are convinced, your job will become easier.

10.9.4   Communicate Risks Early

You must keep pondering and communicating to the customer the impact of risks on the project. Keep the customer informed about your strategy for mitigating these risks. Get a strong stance when you need help from the customer side.

If you sweep risks under the rug and do not communicate properly, then by the time that risk starts creeping in and affecting your project, you will face a lot of flak for not taking a proactive approach.

You should always highlight problem areas of the project to the customer. Customers will always appreciate your honesty. This will also build a trusting relationship with the customer.

This will also help you when any conflict arises. You can show the early warnings you had communicated and thus you can avoid becoming the fall guy.

10.9.5   Commit Less and Deliver More

Never be overzealous in taking additional assignments. It is always a better policy to commit less and deliver more. If the customer is pushing for any extra responsibility, then first assess your situation to see if you can deliver it. If it is not possible, then a firm no is appropriate. You should also do your homework to say why it is not possible. At best you can say that this request can be accommodated in the next release or next assignment.

If it is comfortable for you to deliver something before schedule or something more than what was promised by your side, then the customer will be more than delighted and will acknowledge it. But if you committed something but could not deliver, then it will not be taken lightly.

10.9.6   Be Cool and Share Lighter Moments

Good leaders are the ones who keep their cool even in tough times. So even though your projects always have deadlines approaching and you have tough times in delivering, never lose your cool. Whenever appropriate, share lighter moments with customers. On many occasions this will help you to break the ice with the customer.

10.9.7   Stick to SLAs

Often customers will make service requests that are not part of the original agreement. If you can deliver it, then it is fine. Otherwise always keep your eyes on meeting the SLAs. If you slip on any SLA, then it will be difficult for you to explain why that SLA was not fulfilled.

Bibliography

1. The Standish Group. 1995. Chaos report. http://net.educause.edu/ir/library/pdf/NCP08083B.pdf. Accessed on November 12, 2008.

Chapter 11

Software Testing Practice and Offshoring

Global forces have changed the way business is conducted today. These same forces will change the way business will be conducted tomorrow.

Just 50 years back, most businesses were limited to small geographic locations. Most of them had a presence in one or more cities. Some bigger businesses were doing business in more than one state and sometimes doing business in some other countries as well. But most had a presence within one state alone.

With computers enabling companies to do their businesses in any geographic area and in as many locations as they wanted, companies have grown enormously and have become truly global. They do their marketing in locations where they find good markets for their products, source goods from locations where they find cheaper goods, and manufacture goods where labor costs are cheapest. At the same time they also try to utilize economy of scales opportunities whenever possible.

The software industry has also followed this global trend. Bigger software vendors market their products worldwide, and software development is done at locations where software engineers come cheaper. With more sophistication achieved in the software outsourcing industry, software testing is now very much decoupled from software development. So software testing is being done at locations where labor cost is low yet software testing processes are well developed and thus a thorough testing of the product is possible at cheaper costs. This also helps in achieving lower costs of software maintenance over the life of the software product. Due to the growth in specialization, many service providers have come up who provide excellent software testing services.

In the initial years IT projects were outsourced to service providers who specialized in specific software development expertise like Web enablement, e-commerce enablement, e-business, and so on. But these service providers were from the same host countries and were located near customer sites. So this trend was not leveraging cheap labor. They were offering flexible workforce opportunities. They also provided a skilled workforce.

When every business house in the same industry starts using the same strategy, the advantage for any single company that uses that strategy wanes over time. As can be seen from an analysis of companies, pioneers adopt any strategy early, but if the industry consists of agile competitors (this is true in the case of the software industry where investment in capital goods is not required and any company can change its strategy without much costs), then laggards also catch up fast and the differentiation factor vanishes quickly. To be successful in the marketplace, any business house must have some strategy that is different from its competitors and stick to this strategy until even laggards catch up and the differentiation factor wanes. After the benefits of onshore service providers were utilized to the maximum, the strategic importance of this strategy waned over time and customers started looking for more cost benefits. To utilize this opportunity some offshore service providers came up. Customers had started looking at locations where labor costs were cheaper and where software development could be done at cheaper rates. This trend was also followed due to a shortage of skilled labor within host countries. There were also factors like faster go-to-market needs, flexibility in terms of flexible manpower requirements, right skills required for the project, and so on. Offshoring has provided a lot of advantages in meeting these needs of parent companies. Offshoring is also the answer for the current global business recession. In fact, the world is going to witness business recessions in the future more often due to many factors like global warming, economic slowdown due to the credit crunch, saturating markets, aging of populations, and so on. Software vendors and end users of software are equally facing the problem of continually reduced budgets for IT and software spending. In this situation offshoring is the right answer. It enables software vendors to keep developing their products at the same pace or even at a faster pace than they have been developing their software products and addressing new business issues through adding new features in their software products at significantly lower costs. End users benefit because even with smaller budgets, they are able to get IT systems implemented in time or even before time as implementation costs get reduced substantially and at the same time get more resources to work on projects at substantially lower costs, which helps in reducing project schedules.

With IT projects including software development, software testing, software support, software implementation, business analysis, management analysis, IT-enabled services, and many such processes being offshored, the next trend is providing specialized services for clients.

The current trend is that software service providers are offering dedicated services like software testing services for embedded systems, testing services for enterprise systems, testing services for products being developed, testing services for systems already in production, and so on.

Software testing offshoring provides outstanding benefits like significantly lower costs, improved quality, and speedier go-to-market benefits for software products. Processes for successful offshoring have already been refined, as many software service providers have been in this business for a long time and have gone through the steep learning curve. Their standardized and benchmarked processes ensure consistency across projects, meaningfully utilize the body of knowledge gathered from all previous projects, efficiently utilize labor, and thus provide very high quality service at lower costs and at reduced schedules.

11.1 Challenges

So you want to take advantage of offshoring for your software testing projects. How can you do that? What issues might you have to consider? Is the service provider you are choosing up to it? Are you sure that the relationship is going to work?

There will be a number of questions in your mind, as well as that of your customer, which need to be addressed. How can these issues be resolved?

These challenges can be tackled by having a good checklist and getting correct answers for these questions and then doing your evaluation on these answers. You can provide these checklists along with your answers to your customer so that he is also confident of the outsourcing deal with you.

So here is the checklist that you can use to evaluate your options when you are going to get your customer's project offshored.

11.1.1 Customer Concerns

11.1.1.1 Commercial Concerns

- Concern 1: What is the strategy for your customer to offshore his projects? Will he be outsourcing his entire test organization, just a single project, or just a single task on a single project?
  - Mitigation strategy: Whatever the scenario, be prepared to show your commitment to the relationship by showing how you can help your customer by doing this task on his behalf. Most customers do not outsource everything. They keep some development and testing work with themselves. In all cases customers keep the controlling aspect of the outsourced projects themselves.
- Concern 2: Does your customer want to outsource to reduce headcount or to augment his expertise?

- Mitigation strategy: Clearly controlling the project is always with the customer, and there will be somebody from the customer's side doing it. If the customer's company needs training or to develop expertise, then you need to provide appropriate training and help them to acquire expertise. If, on the other hand, the customer is looking to reduce their headcount, then you need to sit with the customer to chalk out detailed transitioning of the project.

■ Concern 3: Will outsourcing be used to fulfill a legal/contractual obligation of independent testing or for satisfying your customer's own requirements?

■ Mitigation strategy: In case of contractual obligation, you will need to familiarize yourself with the legal and commercial aspects of the obligation of your customer to incorporate it into your offering. In the other case, you just need to satisfy all explicit and implicit requirements of your customer. Even with small engagements, offshoring introduces many complexities in the project, including cultural differences, changed time zones, productivity differences, different perceptions, different work ethics, language barriers, great distance, different organization structures, different roles, changed stakeholder expectations, and so on.

11.1.1.2 Technical and Process Concerns

■ Concern 1: Do you feel that expectations from your customer are unrealistic regarding cost, schedule, or quality goals?

- Mitigation strategy: How are you going to present realistic project plans to your customer? How are you going to convince your customer about schedules, price, and quality expectations? Especially when automation of testing is part of the project, expectations are high for unrealistic schedules. Mitigation of such unrealistic goals should be the top priority for the outsourcer. Prepare yourself for this.

■ Concern 2: Customer has a deep concern for the ability of the offshore partner to execute projects. He is not sure whether his partner's team has any understanding of the subject matter related to the product on which they have to work. Can the team get up and running quickly on the specific product to be built? Is the team well conversant on the technology used in building the application? Can the team integrate quickly with his development process? Can the team understand his specific needs?

- Mitigation strategy: It is a fact that the more distance between the customer and his partner, the less confidence the customer has over the ability of his partner to execute his projects. This is the most serious concern the customer has. You need to present your prior similar work experience with other customers and the skill sets of your employees who will be working on this project. You will need to explain your delivery model to the customer. You will need to show your expertise in working from remote locations. You may have to thoroughly explain the benefits of this model and how the onshore + offshore model will work. One more important task is to align your processes to match processes followed by your customer. Even if you are a CMM5-level company, aligning your processes is a big challenge for you.

■ Concern 3: When teams work from remote locations and belong to different organizations (especially in the customer-partner environment), a lot of documentation is needed about the product to be developed and the process to be followed. This leads to more costs and labor. To keep costs in check, most of the customers decide to restrict the project size by cutting the development of many features. This situation also leads to reduced discussion on further development of these features.

■ Mitigation strategy: There will be initial costs involved in any outsourcing deal such as additional documentation costs. But these costs are paid off in the long term. Offshoring can save costs more than 70% over a 3-year period and even more in the longer run. Nowadays most of the outsourcers have very flexible processes that can be changed easily, so switching from one outsourcer to another is easy. It is very important for you to convince your customer that offshoring benefits are gained only in the long term. Benefits also result when a proper transitioning approach including a piloting phase and knowledge transfer is done properly.

11.1.1.3 Legal Concerns

■ Concern 1: The customer and the outsourcing partner may lack prior contracting experience, which may result in lopsided or impractical contracting agreements.
  - Mitigation strategy: Lack of contracting experience from any side definitely poses a serious threat to the project. To mitigate the risk, the contracting should start at a small scale. Once contracting experience increases and the confidence level of all parties increases, bigger contracts can be looked at.

■ Concern 2: Many outsourcing companies try to promise too much in order to bag the contract. Sometimes this could also be due to cultural differences in presentation and self-perception of expertise.
  - Mitigation strategy: The best measure to find out if the outsourcer is promising too much is to dig through your schedules for previous projects and extrapolate to find out if schedules made by your outsourcer are realistic. Better yet, engage an impartial consultant who can evaluate and judge if schedules are realistic.

■ Concern 3: Customers have strong reservations against potential for security leaks, loss of intellectual property rights, conflicts of interest, and so on. These reservations are further exacerbated by cultural differences.

- Mitigation strategy: These kinds of risks can best be checked by framing elaborate legal contracts outlining the responsibility and authority of each party in the agreement. There should be agreements such as penalties for any breach of conduct and a noncompete clause. I remember one incident when, due to the negligence of the outsourcing company's employees, customer data was lost from a database just before the start of peak Thanksgiving season. Employees of the outsourcing company were not allowed to access the production database as per service level agreements but, not adhering to the agreements, the customer gave the employee access. So the original problem was from the customer side itself. They should not have given access to the database to the outsourcing company in the first place.

■ Concern 4: Many customers report that the performance standards of their offshoring partner are not clear to them. Sometimes they are not able to understand or use these reports in a meaningful manner. They also report that costing for the work done is not clear to them.

- Mitigation strategy: These kinds of risks can best be checked by framing good service level agreements and following strict compliance to these agreements. There should be clearly defined deliverables with clear sign-off dates for deliveries. The milestones must be set. All of the activities in performing tasks during the project must be defined clearly. There should be clear methodology for effort estimation and costing for each head of expenses defined.

■ Concern 5: Many customers have complaints about poor risk planning by the offshoring partner.

- Mitigation strategy: These kinds of risks can best be checked by providing for appropriate buffer for measurable or immeasurable risks. The testing process should also be agile enough to take care of unexpected events.

■ Concern 6: Many customers have complaints that the conflict resolution process is poorly defined.

- Mitigation strategy: Alongside the service level agreements, there should also be a provision for agreeable settlement in case of disputes and conflicts. For instance, many times it may happen that the deliveries made by the outsourcing partner are not satisfactory as per the expectation of the customer. In such instances, there should be provision for rework.

To convince the customer over these concerns, you again may need to show success stories from your past projects. You may need to back your proposal with your defined processes that are assessed at any software engineering measurement standard like ISO9001, CMMI, or PCMMI.

11.2   Benefits of Offshoring

Doubts and uncertainties aside, let us discuss how offshoring your software testing project can benefit you. Let us look at a case study. In this case study, first a traditional approach to software testing is studied for an American company. Then a

Figure 11.1   Traditional approach to software testing.

service provider is contracted to offshore testing projects first on a pilot basis and then under a thorough program over a period of 3 years. Cost analysis, schedule analysis, and other factors are discussed in detail in the process of dissecting this approach.

11.2.1   Traditional Approach to Testing

Software testing always used to be considered as an afterthought in most software development projects due to the fact that software developers used to operate in sellers markets. There were always eager buyers available who were willing to buy substandard software products. So quality control was never a priority area during software development. As a result, software testing used to happen at the fag end of software development projects just before deployment. As you can see in Figure 11.1, it was just a phase in the entire process.

But with an increasing number of players in the market, things started changing. Now buyers had more options. This necessitated the software vendors to improve the quality of their products. So slowly software testing started gaining prominence. Now, more and more, software testing aspects were getting integrated into the entire software life cycle.

In the traditional software development model, testing teams got involved too late in the software life cycle. This limited their ability to provide accurate and comprehensive test coverage. This also used to result in inadequate effort estimation, which used to result in delayed delivery and budget overruns. Software testing was mostly an ad hoc exercise, and no formal processes or metrics were established. This used to result in a limited ability to measure and improve efficiency and effort. There was a problem that quality assurance and testing were not considered specialized skills or career path but rather peripheral activities in software development. Due to this, developers used to test their own code and top talent used to move out of software quality roles. This led to a situation in which unqualified resources were recruited who used to perform and manage testing activities.

11.2.2   Cost of Late Detection of Defects

In Chapter 1 we discussed that the later a defect is detected in the software life cycle, the costlier it gets to fix. This is why it is very important that quality assurance and software testing should start as early in the project as possible. Software testing should not only find defects after the software coding is done and the system build is made but also contribute to all phases of the software life cycle.

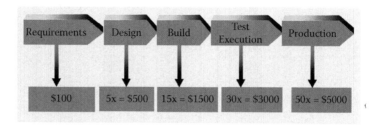

Figure 11.2   Cost of late detection of defects in traditional software development model.

For this to happen, organization structure and roles need to be changed. (See Figures 11.2 and 11.3.)

11.3   Proposed Organization Structure

As the testing function needs to be taken to a level where it can be integrated with all processes and phases of the software life cycle, there is a need to think about all aspects and areas of changes needed. Change management is an elaborate subject and is beyond the scope of this book. However, we will discuss what new structure should be in place for process management, methodology, tools and technology management, infrastructure needed, and delivery model.

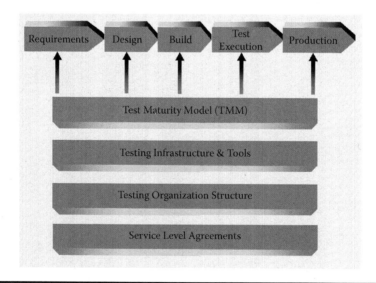

Figure 11.3   New approach to software testing.

11.3.1 Process Structure

Modern-day software test projects require a proven, quality-driven process framework that promotes quality of work as well as checkpoints in the process model for associated costs. Knowledge and experience bring innovation for project work, whereas a mature process framework brings exceptional quality of work. In fact, without a good and standard process framework, it is difficult to execute large and complex test projects, as people working at geographically remote locations will not be able to communicate effectively. The new model should support processes such as code promotion, build acceptance, defect management, test bed management, test execution reporting, knowledge management, tracking of project metrics, and quality initiatives throughout the test life cycle.

11.3.2 Project Components

Components for the outsourced offshore projects should include test planning and estimation, requirements traceability, integration testing, system testing, user acceptance testing, performance testing, regression testing, test data creation, automation testing, etc. The comprehensive process and project management framework allows for systematic project work with assured quality of work. Using best practices and common processes that are available within these frameworks, it is possible to achieve the same level of quality across all projects for all customer accounts.

11.3.3 Infrastructure

People are the most important assets for software test projects. Nevertheless, without infrastructure, projects cannot be executed. Tools and infrastructure allow for easy and fast communication, better productivity, and better quality. Infrastructure becomes more important in case of teams located at many distant sites, as affordable and reliable communication devices are critical for smooth functioning of the project. Infrastructure required for delivering test projects includes staging environments, test beds, desktops, networks, communication devices, discussion boards, and so on.

11.3.4 Tools

Tools are one of the components of any project; the use of tools improves the productivity of team members of the project. To use a tool, team members must possess the knowledge and experience of using that tool. If team members are not familiar with the tool, then even if it is a good tool, it will not result in a significant productivity increase. On the other hand, a poor tool will result in productivity loss instead of productivity gain. So it is vital that the right tools are selected for the project. To enable the project teams to be more productive and share information easily, good tools and technology are required. Some of the tools for test projects should include test management tools, performance appraisal tools, test automation tools, requirements management tools, templates, and other tools.

11.3.5 Operating Model

In outsourcing projects, service level agreements (SLAs) govern all aspects of projects. At the same time, applying shared knowledge and common standard processes ensures uniform quality across projects. So applying these common standard processes on top of individual service level agreements is crucial to achieve consistent and uniform quality for all projects. Processes in the operating model include project structuring, staff assignments, workload management, organizational SLAs, and so on.

11.3.6 Organization

Excellence in providing world-class services requires good work culture and mature and well-defined processes. The proposed model requires an excellent delivery model as well as efficient and quality processes to govern all projects. A new delivery model calls for an entirely new organizational structure including center of excellence facilities for specialized tasks, matrix organization structure, skills availability matrix, changed organization structure, training programs, professional certifications, career path options for talented and hardworking individuals, and so on.

11.4 Software Testing Consolidation

As we have discussed in a previous section, software testing in a software development project used to be on an ad hoc basis, had no standard process definition, and lacked clarity, which resulted in poor quality, budget, and schedule escalation. A testing team was attached to each software development project. These testing teams had no relation to each other and had their own methodology, process, tools, and team structure, which were entirely different from one team to another. This resulted in inefficiency and uneven quality across projects (see Table 11.1).

Table 11.1 Traditional Software Testing Approach

Business Unit 1	Business Unit 2	Business Unit 3
Development team	Development team	Development team
Testers	Testers	Testers

Table 11.2   New Software Testing Approach with Testing Consolidation

Business Unit 1	Business Unit 2	Business Unit 3
Development team	Development team	Development team
Centralized quality group		

To rectify things, we can form a centralized quality group that can handle all projects for all customers. In this scheme of things, resources, tools, and technology can be shared across all projects. At the same time, the same process and methodology will ensure that quality and efficiency across all projects will be the same. So, on one hand, we will have lower costs due to sharing of resources and, on the other hand, we will have uniform quality (see Table 11.2).

11.5   Advantages of Offshoring Coupled with Centralized Quality Group

Setting a project team to execute a software development project and adding software testing resources to this team is no longer a good business model. It does not provide good business value. The best option is to use an offshoring partner whose expertise, resources, infrastructure, and new delivery model will provide the best benefits. This model provides cost savings, mature processes that result in better quality, better project control, better metrics measurements, strict SLA compliance, expert services for testing management, test automation, and so on. This model also provides flexible resource management.

11.5.1   Offshore Team Structure

For this model to work, the organization structure must provide a facility to share resources, use expertise from expertise groups (called center of excellence), adopt mature methodologies like Capability Maturity Model Integration (CMMI), and share infrastructure. It should allow for shared use of tools.

There should be a provision to have dedicated teams on projects as well as flexible additional teams so that this extra manpower can be deployed whenever needed.

11.6   Case Study

This case study is taken from an engagement with a midsize U.S. software vendor. They had their own software testing team that used to test all deployed and under-development software applications. Due to market conditions, they decided to outsource a part of their software testing function to an offshore service provider. Because it was a new business model for them, they decided to start the engagement with a pilot project and then gradually go for the full-fledged contract. The study is done for a 3-year period starting from the pilot.

11.6.1   The Current State Scenario

The customer has a 45-person testing team, comprising 30 full-time employees and 15 contractors. Salary for testing team members is $80,000 per year and that for contractors is $100,000 per year. Annual voluntary attrition is 5%, with the average cost of replacement cost equivalent to 3 months' salary and benefits. The customer has implemented some automation with about 20% of functional test cases being automated.

11.6.2   The Future State Scenario

The customer decided to retain 10% of its internal and contract resources for testing. Thirty percent of the workforce will be eliminated and the remaining 60% of internal full-time employees will be reassigned to other tasks within the organization.

In the proposed new scheme of things, 70% of the service provider's team would form the fixed team, while an additional 30% capacity would ramp up cyclically every 6 months. About 10 to 15% of the service provider's team will be on-site and the remaining 85 to 90% of the team will be at an offshore location. The knowledge transfer and piloting would last for a quarter, with a 12-person team (6 on-site, 6 offshore). In a 3-year period, the service provider's team will achieve an overall 15% improvement in efficiency compared to efficiency levels in the current situation. Total resource requirements would drop year after year based on automation and efficiency gains. (See Table 11.3.)

Table 11.3   Existing Internal Testing Labor Costs

	Year 1	Year 2	Year 3	Total
Full-time employees costs × 30	$2,400,000.00	$2,400,000.00	$2,400,000.00	$7,200,000.00
Testing contractors costs × 15	$1,500,000.00	$1,500,000.00	$1,500,000.00	$4,500,000.00
Voluntary attrition costs	$60,000.00	$60,000.00	$60,000.00	$180,000.00
Total costs	$3,960,000.00	$3,960,000.00	$3,960,000.00	$11,880,000.00

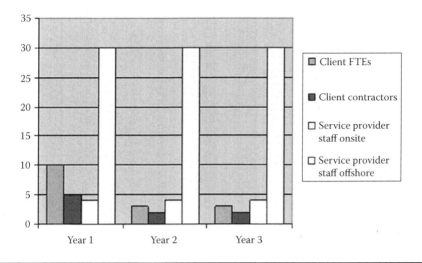

Figure 11.4 Average annual staff strength for 3 years.

11.6.3 A 3-Year Labor Cost ROI Scenario

With the introduction of a new model, average total staffing for the first year is 49 (10 customer's full-time employees + 5 contractors + 30 offshore and 4 on-site employees of the service provider) compared to 45 internal staff before the engagement. In the second and third years, average staffing will drop to 39. Many employees of the service provider will be working on many projects of the customer applications. These employees are attached to center of excellence facilities. So their workload is divided across many projects (see Figure 11.4).

11.6.4 Challenge

The real challenge for which the new model was needed was that the customer was in dire need of reducing operating costs. At the same time, they were looking to achieve higher efficiency and better quality. They were also looking to have a consistent quality across all of their projects. Even though the top leadership of the customer had mandated continuous process improvement, the customer's own facilities and resources lacked tools and environment to achieve this top priority goal.

11.6.5 Solution

To face the challenge, the service provider established an offshore Central Quality Group to deliver software testing services to the customer, structured around SLAs. They selected the team that would go on-site at the customer's location and start transitioning of the project. They worked with the existing customer's project team to take charge. They first learned all aspects of the project from the internal team. They also started transferring the knowledge to the offshore team. In the 3-month pilot, they took three applications to successfully transition to the offshore team. Once the pilot was successful, the full-capacity offshore team took charge. They took the remaining projects from the customer's internal team and started delivering on a full scale. The customer benefited immensely from the service provider's mature methodology, which was based on CMMI guidelines, along with the knowledge gained in executing similar projects in the past. This resulted in better quality of the software applications. Due to the centralized testing service, all projects started having uniform quality. Due to lower costs at the offshore location, costs were reduced substantially.

11.6.6 New Model Implementation Details

The service provider built a dedicated 40-person team to operate within enterprise and project level SLAs. For this engagement, the service provider established well-defined software testing processes and developed process road maps, estimation models, automation standards, and so on. The final outcome was that postproduction defects got reduced through structured requirements analysis and full traceability to test cases. The regression test cycle schedule got reduced by automating test cases using QTP. Increased visibility to testing and development activities was achieved through comprehensive metrics collection and reporting (see Table 11.4).

11.6.7 Pilot Project Details

The service provider's team validated and fine-tuned the process model to suit the requirements of the customer in the pilot. The team learned to use the automation tool on specific tasks in the project. They introduced standard metrics available

Table 11.4 Applications Offshored per Quarter

Q1	Q2	Q3	Q4
Application 1	Application 4	Application 10	Application 16
Application 2	Application 5	Application 11	Application 17
Application 3	Application 6	Application 12	Application 18
	Application 7	Application 13	Application 19
	Application 8	Application 14	Application 20
	Application 9	Application 15	

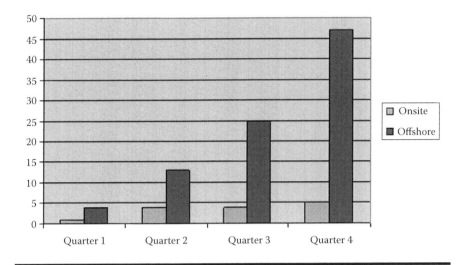

Figure 11.5   Service provider staff strength for first four quarters.

with a central quality group to be used for the pilot. The team also brought subject matter experts to take high-level domain and technology requirements for the project (see Figure 11.5).

11.6.8   Process Model

There has been a lot of discussion about which process model fits well to what kind of software project. The reality is that even if you have implemented a well-defined and refined process model, all tasks on a project need more details than the guidelines outlined in these process models. Software testing is such a specific activity where models are still evolving. There is always a debate about whether one should follow the waterfall model or go for an iterative approach.

These arguments can go on and on, but people who are associated with different kinds of approaches for adopting process models will vouch for a suitable model for each project.

In a central quality center approach, things are totally different. We are talking of not one project but a lot of projects. We are talking of shared resources and a rich pool of expertise to be tapped for each project. We are talking of providing a standard platform for all projects so that uniform quality is attained, and at the same time, due to adherence to mature processes, better quality could be achieved on all projects.

In the standard process adopted by the service provider for all of the projects for all customers, the process steps were engagement/initiation, knowledge transfer, test planning and estimation, test design, automation script creation using keyword-driven framework, test execution cycle, analysis and reporting, archiving of project details, and finally preparation for the next release (see Figure 11.6).

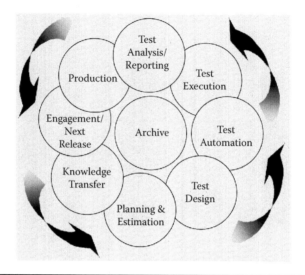

Figure 11.6   Process model.

Even though there will be sign-offs at each milestone, the process is adaptable enough to allow for agility. For instance, the model is well suited for incremental iterations for product development.

11.6.9   Benefits of New Model

Benefits of the new model include increase in productivity and quality, reduction in costs and schedules, and ability to provide a platform for consolidation of many projects.

11.6.9.1   Productivity

Model features that help in improving productivity include round-the-clock (different time zones help here) testing model leading to reduction in test cycle time; automated regression testing, which reduces regression testing cycle time; quick ramp-up and ramp-down of resources, which increases resource flexibility; perfectly synchronized on-site/offshore setup; one-stop shop for providing dedicated resources for various Central Quality Group technology needs; and skilled automation resources.

11.6.9.2   Quality

Model features that help in improving quality include assurance of business requirements; proven and unique methodology for testing; usage of automation tools; continuous process improvements; high test case coverage; and SEI–CMMI Level 5 certified processes.

11.6.9.3   Cost

Model features that help in reducing costs include flexible staffing based on resource load variations; higher cost reduction due to low on-site ratio and major team staff based at low-cost location; and high automation gains.

11.6.10   Automation Benefits

Some of the testing processes that can be successfully automated include test management, test case execution, test analysis, and reporting. Even here test case execution cannot be automated completely. So most testing activities are predominantly manual and are not readily amenable to automation. However, automation offers advantages over manual efforts. It reduces or eliminates human error, reduces monotonous work from human beings, helps in bringing in reusable components that increase productivity, and reduces execution time substantially.

The kind of application being tested, the automation tool used, the kind of testing required, and the kind of test cases to be automated dictate how much automation can and should be done. Automation for test case execution requires extra work in the form of creating scripts. So automation is useful only when the test case being automated should be run repeatedly. It will be waste if a test case that is required to run only once or twice is being automated. Regression test cases are supposed to run many times over different releases of the software. So these test cases are the best candidates for automation. Similarly, in the production instance, sanity test cases are run repeatedly. So these are also good candidates for automation (see Figure 11.7).

The team was able to automate almost 99% of regression and sanity test cases. The chosen tool (QTP and LoadRunner) came in handy as this feature-rich tool really helped in automating test cases efficiently without much manual coding in scripts. Overall the team was able to automate almost 66% of all test cases (functional, performance, compatibility, and integration) across all 23 applications and all versions of these applications.

Variation in percentage of automation will depend on complexity of test cases in any project. In the engagement, the team found some test cases that were very

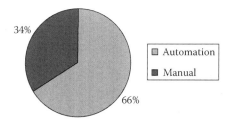

Figure 11.7   Automation of test execution out of total testing effort.

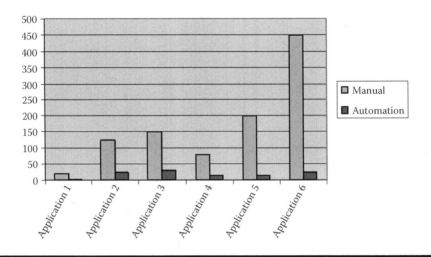

Figure 11.8   Time required in executing manual vs. automated test cases for each application.

complex and the automation effort required was very steep. So the team decided not to automate them.

Due to automation, effort reduction in test case execution was to the tune of 85% for one application. On average, effort reduction came in at 76%. In Figure 11.8 times required in manual test execution and automated test execution for the same test cases for some applications are depicted. You can see that time required has shrunk considerably. In Figure 11.9 this shrinkage is shown in percentage figures.

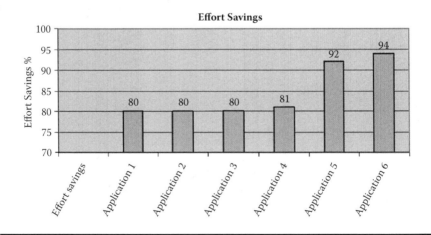

Figure 11.9   Time savings due to automation.

This reduction in time savings is crucial. In product development cycles, product vendors release major versions of their software on a quarterly basis. As is well known, these software products have grown manifold over the last 10 years. Product vendors have been adding new features in the products regularly. Whenever a new version is to be released, all the existing features of the software have to be tested to make sure that any modifications or extensions done in old features or changes due to addition of new features do not affect the functionality of these features. To accomplish this, regression testing is done with all releases. The suite of regression test cases keeps increasing with addition/modification of features. So time required to execute these test cases keep increasing with new releases. This leads to a delay in the release of new versions. By automating these test cases, time required gets reduced substantially over executing regression test cases manually. In some cases this reduction is more than 90%.

In this case study, the customer benefited immensely by automation of regression test cases, as it allowed the customer to release new versions much faster. The time savings on some applications came to more than 10 working days, which is substantial for a quarterly release.

11.6.10.1   Key Highlights

Some of the highlights of the automation testing included 66% automation of test case execution and management, mercury tools used for automation, traceability matrix maintained, module-centric approach followed to minimize maintenance effort, reusable components to be used across projects using keyword-driven framework, common standards across all projects, trained and certified professionals, and time and cost savings during regression testing.

11.6.10.2   Sanity Testing

Sanity test cases on the production instance were executed on a daily basis. They were automated completely by the service provider's team. They were also run automatically at certain times of the day. Result of the executed sanity test was sent automatically to support staff. On some applications, it took more than 1 hour to run all sanity tests. Performance regression test cases as well as functional regression test cases were part of the sanity tests (see Figure 11.10).

Sanity tests were run nightly so that the application was available for testing when no users were using the applications; as a result, testing activities did not interfere with users' activities. If any problems were detected, they were communicated to the support team, who acted swiftly to rectify them. This ensured that by the time users started using the application at 9 a.m., the problems were fixed and did not affect any users (see Figure 11.11).

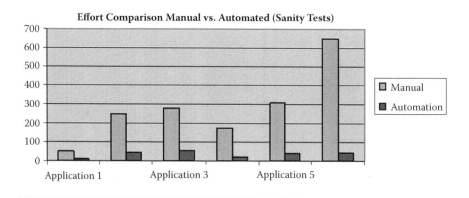

Figure 11.10   Effort comparison for manual vs. automated tests for sanity.

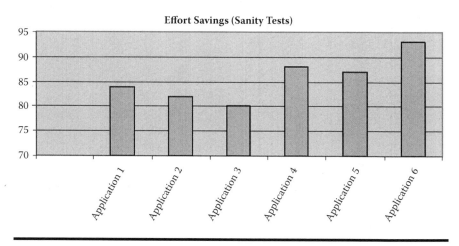

Figure 11.11   Effort savings for manual vs. automated tests for sanity.

Automated sanity tests also became extremely useful for the customer. Earlier, running these tests manually used to involve a team of five people at night, which used to take more than 4 hours for each application. Now, no staff is required as these tests are completely automated and run automatically at specific times during the night.

Chapter 12

Software Testing as a Commodity

So your software testing is offshored and you reap all the benefits.

So far so good! Your competitors have also done the same. Now what? Where do you go from here?

Here comes an enlightening thought: What if I find an offshore partner who can reduce my testing costs further somehow with the same schedule and quality? Is it possible? What will it take? Well! Here is a solution.

Before mass manufacturing was introduced, society was consuming goods that were manufactured at small manufacturing sites. Raw material was procured from local sources. Most of the manufacturing was labor-intensive. A few simple machines were deployed in manufacturing. Produced goods were consumed by local customers.

Compare this scenario with the service sector as it exists in our contemporary society. The service sector today is labor-intensive. Some automation and IT devices are used, but still most of the work is performed through labor effort. No raw material is required in services. Services are consumed not only by local customers but also by customers located within a wide geographic area (see Figure 12.1).

When mass manufacturing was introduced, many of the erstwhile barriers were removed. Raw material was now procured globally or at least from within a wide geographic area. Quantity of sourced material increased manifold. More and more machines were now deployed in manufacturing. Manufacturing sites started producing goods on a large scale. Machines were also getting sophisticated and became more productive over time. Labor effort got reduced. Produced goods were consumed by global customers (see Figure 12.2).

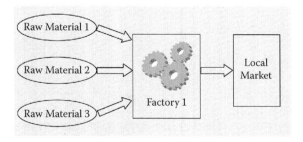

Figure 12.1   Traditional manufacturing.

Mass manufacturing brought many benefits to society. Manufacturers started sourcing goods from places where they could get raw material cheaper. This helped in decreasing manufacturing costs, which resulted in lower prices for these goods for the customers. Operating costs were substantially reduced due to reduction in labor effort. This also resulted in achieving lower manufacturing costs, which in turn resulted in still lower prices for these goods for the customers. Goods produced by these machines were also of better quality. So consumers benefited by getting better-quality products. Because goods were produced at large scale, it was possible to send them to wide geographic areas so that a large section of society was able to consume them.

Overall, mass production introduced a huge improvement and society benefited immensely. By commoditizing goods, costs were lowered, quality was improved, and a large section of society was able to consume goods.

Can the same kind of revolution be achieved in the services sector?

Yes! It is possible.

In this chapter we will try to investigate in detail whether software testing is a good candidate for becoming a commodity. We can then refer to this phenomenon as "software testing mass services."

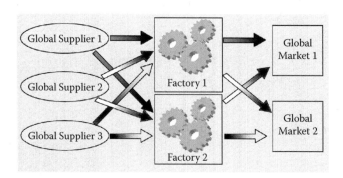

Figure 12.2   Mass manufacturing.

12.1   Software Offshoring

Software services providers have been offshoring software development along with testing projects offshore. Customers reap the benefits of lower labor cost, consistent quality, and reduced schedules. Service providers also leverage their knowledge of executing similar projects in the past, which helps new projects.

So far, offshoring has provided benefits like consolidation, sharing of resources, better utilization of resources, lower costs, and excellence due to strict adherence to software engineering principles and software process standards like CMMI.

The time has come for something more to be done than what has been achieved through offshoring.

12.2   The New Concept

Offshore service providers execute a lot of projects simultaneously. They can put these projects into categories. Similar projects are in the same category. They can create central organizations called centers of excellence (CoE) for providing specialized services. So we can have a CoE for QTP automation, another CoE for LoadRunner performance automation, and yet another CoE for creating test cases for CRM (customer relationship management) applications. So, on the one hand, we have processing centers and, on the other hand, we can have lines for services. This will be similar to production lines in manufacturing industries.

We can see that mass services already exist in the form of call centers, bill generation, and so on. Software testing can be set up along similar lines.

There will be a central department that will receive incoming projects. Each project will be analyzed and will be broken into parts. These parts will be sent to concerned CoEs. The CoEs will process these parts and will forward them to the next CoE in line, who in turn will process and then forward them to the next CoE. This continues until processing is complete on that part, and then the part will be considered finished. All the parts will then be assembled by a central organization. So each software test project will be ready to be delivered after this assembly.

During processing, each part of the project will be treated as an inventory item. They will wait in line to be processed when their turn comes. Once processing is done, they are forwarded to the next processing center.

Already you may have a feel for this idea.

Now let us describe the process in detail.

12.2.1   Old Organization Structure

As has been traditionally done, software testing is an integral part of any software project. In the software development life cycle, there is a phase for testing when all testing for the application is done. In such an arrangement, the testing phase is handled by a software testing team that is led by a software testing lead or test manager. For automation testing, there could be team members who are automation engineers and who will be building automation scripts for the test cases that are to be automated. There are functional experts who have industry knowledge and who will do the majority of functionality testing. There will be experts who will do performance testing of the application using automation tools.

With outsourcing of software testing, these organization arrangements get changed significantly.

From the client side, there will be a project manager who oversees the engagements with service providers. Under him, there will be a small team who look after managing software development and software testing done by internal staff as well as by service providers.

The topmost position from the service provider side is the engagement or delivery or account manager who is responsible for all communication, clarification, and deliverables for all projects that are getting executed for that specific client. Under him, there could be a project manager for software development and under *him* will be a software testing manager to take care of software testing functions.

12.2.2   New Organization Structure

Software testing, as is now well known, should never be confined to just one phase of software development. Instead testing activities should be spread across all phases of software development.

If this is the case, then how are we going to integrate software testing parts with other parallel software development activities? These software development activities will be going on at different locations and will be done by other organizations with whom the service provider who has undertaken software testing may not have any connections.

In the new model, software testing function is detached from the software development function, and in the extreme case software testing is done by an altogether different organization that have connections with the organization that will be doing software development. Software testing thus becomes a separate project, distinct from the software development project. In fact, the organization that will be doing the software testing will offer its software testing expertise as a mass service to reduce project costs and offer its testing services to its customers at lower prices. However, this type of arrangement posses a communications problem for the organization doing the software development project and the one which is doing the software testing project. There are many touch points between these two projects. If these two projects are being done by two separate companies, then how can proper communication between these companies be nesured? We will discuss the solution for this problem later in Section 12.3.

Let us first see a traditional organizational structure (see Figures 12.3 and 12.4). It can be seen that the organization structure needed by the service provider for software testing management becomes very complex in this new scenario. He needs delivery managers who work closely with the customer. A delivery manager may be working with

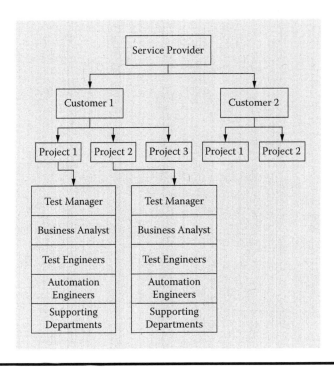

Figure 12.3   Organization structure for traditional service provider.

more than one customer at the same time. He gets the project details and approaches CoEs for the work to be done on the project. These CoEs can be organized by the service provider on the basis of his needs. Suppose the service provider has customers who have Oracle application implementations as well as customers who have SAP implemented.

In this scenario we can have the following options to form CoE:

1. Form CoEs based on functional expertise (e.g., finance, customer relationship management, supply chain management, manufacturing).
2. Form CoEs based on application. So we can have CoE for Oracle applications, CoE for SAP, and so on.
3. Form matrix CoEs. In this case we can have a larger CoE for, say, manufacturing, and inside the larger organization we can have smaller segments organized by application (e.g., Oracle applications or SAP).

Matrix organization is the best-suited solution. So we can have automation engineers who specialize in writing script using QTP. These engineers can be placed in either SAP or Oracle applications CoE. This structure is good because it facilitates switching resources from one CoE to another without spending much money on training.

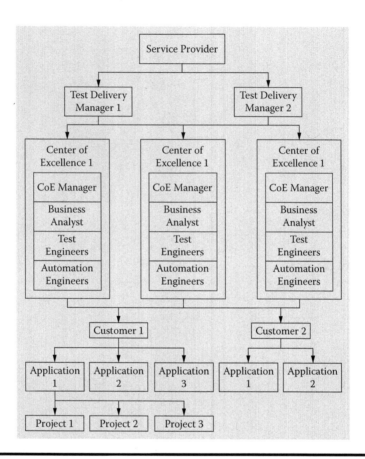

Figure 12.4   Organization structure for pathbreaking service provider.

One solution could be to organize testing based on these practices as is traditionally done. So we can have one CoE for Oracle applications and one CoE for SAP. But we can see that there will be duplication of resources. For instance, we will have a "CoE for QTP automation for Oracle practice" and another "QTP automation CoE for SAP." Instead we can just have one CoE for QTP automation, which will serve both Oracle applications practice and SAP practice. In fact it will provide flexibility in team management. When the company has more projects on Oracle Application, more automation engineers will be assigned to these projects, and if there are more projects on SAP, then more automation engineers will be assigned to these SAP projects.

There is one more dimension to it: How can we integrate activities being performed at the testing organization with the activities being carried out at the organization that is engaged in software development?

It can be done by linking the independent test project closely with the development project.

12.3   Linking Test Project with Development Project

It can be seen in Figure 12.5 that the customer outsources development and testing projects to different service providers. When requirements-gathering activities are completed by the development organization, it passes the documents to the testing organization. The testing organization starts preparations for test case design. In the meantime the development organization works on the software architecture and design and delivers the design to the testing organization. The testing organization starts creating test cases and automation scripts. The development team meanwhile starts coding activities and starts builds. The test organization is given access to create a test environment based on the builds. The testing team starts executing test cases on these builds. Here we have two-way communication. The test team reports test case failures and defect information to the development team. The development team fixes those defects and releases new builds for verification. The testing team retests and submits the report. This iteration continues as per agreements. Once this phase is over, the developed software is ready for deployment. Once the software application is deployed, the testing team has two tasks. First, the team must run sanity scripts to check whether the production environment is working properly. This is done on a periodic basis. Second, the team must validate the production environment whenever a patch is applied by the development team on the

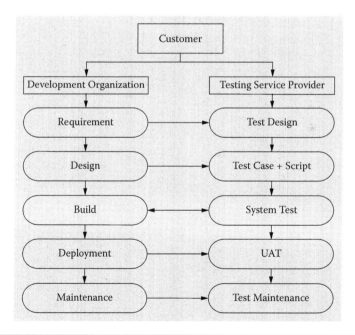

Figure 12.5   Links between customer, development, and testing organization activities.

production environment. There is one aspect to it. Whenever some maintenance is done by development, the test case, automation script, and test data may have to change. These activities are also carried out by the testing team.

For this scheme to work, a tight service level agreement framework will have to be developed, implemented, and agreed upon by all parties. When the development plan or test plan is done, it should be agreed upon by all stakeholders from all sides.

But, once in place, this can bring tremendous benefits to the customer.

12.4   Mass Manufacturing

The outside view of mass manufacturing is essentially mass sourcing to reduce raw material cost, and mass production to reduce the operation costs of manufactured goods.

Let us discuss mass manufacturing concepts. One characteristic is consolidation. Using consolidation, one can reduce manufacturing costs by using resources that are shared for all manufacturing activities. For instance, a good amount of resource processing time is lost in setup and waiting for raw material to arrive. A specific machine can process several types of goods. But machine setup has to change to start processing another kind of goods. For example, a lathe machine is set up to process a certain automobile part. After finishing a batch of these parts, the next batch of parts to be processed is different from the parts in the first batch. So the lathe machine is set up to process these parts now. It takes time to change the setup of a machine. Any machine may need to change setup 10 to 12 times a day. If each setup requires on average 25 minutes, then in a single day the machine is not productive for more than 4 hours.

After processing each part, there is an idle time when the machine waits for the next part to process. Suppose the machine processes 500 parts a day. The waiting time for the next part to arrive at the machine is 30 seconds. So the machine is not productive for more than 4 hours a day.

Now let us discuss one more problem faced by the manufacturing industry. Suppose in the manufacturing process, goods are to be colored at one processing step. Goods are to be colored as per the order. These colors can range from green, red, blue, and darker colors to light colors. Generally when one batch of goods is colored with the same color, the dye has to be changed to another color for the next batch of goods. Generally, if cleaning of the machine is required to remove the color, it takes 24 hours. If the previous color was a light color and the next batch of goods requires a darker color, then this cleaning is not required. But if the previous color was dark and now goods need a lighter color, then the machine has to be cleaned; otherwise the darker color will get smeared on this batch of goods and the goods will get spoiled. For productivity reasons orders should be sorted and then manufacturing planning should be done so that orders containing goods with lighter colors are processed first. Next will be orders having goods with slightly darker colors. This goes on until the darkest-colored goods are processed near the end of the manufacturing planning period. This technique is called *sequencing* of orders.

There is one more concept in mass manufacturing. It is called *pegging*. Any order consists of many order lines. Each order line will have one manufactured good (item) with some quantity required to be delivered by some specific date. The manufacturer determines which raw materials may be needed in manufacturing that item in a certain quantity. These raw materials then go through processing steps. In each processing step, the processed material is known as WIP (work in process) material until it becomes a finished item. For different items, many times the WIP material may be the same. For example, in the steel industry hot iron is the same regardless of any finished product. So the quantity of hot iron needed for all orders can be calculated, and that much hot iron is to be produced in the manufacturing planning period. Similarly, in the textile industry, the kind of thread needed for manufacturing different kinds of clothes may be the same. The amount of thread required for all orders can be calculated and aggregated for orders requiring the same thread. During production, the specific order for which the thread is being produced will not be known. This creates problems in tracking orders. For example, when a customer calls and asks how much more time will be required for his order to be manufactured, the factory may not be able to answer this question. By pegging the WIP to the orders, it is possible to know the order for which the thread is being produced.

Let us see if these manufacturing concepts apply to software testing when it is done as a mass service.

12.4.1 Setup

When a project arrives, the test manager makes a plan for its execution. He plans for configuration management, resource requirements, skill requirements, time required for each activity, and contingency plan for any eventuality. The new project may be vastly different from earlier projects. So he may have to change many things from earlier projects. As a result, planning activity may take some time. When the plan is actually made, tasks are assigned to individual resources. These resources may have to do some preparation before taking up the assignments. The preparation time may be considered the setup time (see Figures 12.6 and 12.7).

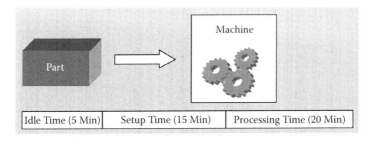

Figure 12.6   Idle, setup, and processing time for a part in manufacturing.

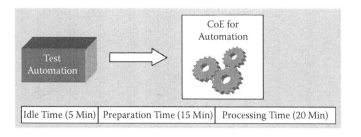

Figure 12.7 Idle, preparation, and processing time for an automation part in software test project.

To reduce preparation time, the test manager should assign tasks closely similar to what the resource was doing earlier. This way the preparation time can be reduced. If the task is exactly the same as the one he was performing, then the preparation time may be completely eliminated.

12.4.2 Idle Time

Resources finish their assignments and then wait for the next assignment to come. This is their idle time.

To reduce idle time, a good database has to be maintained for resource allocation, and it can be queried when a resource becomes available for the next assignment. Accordingly it should be assigned new tasks so that it is not idle at any time.

12.4.3 Sequencing

Tasks of any project carry some kind of priority. Some tasks are not so urgent and can be kept in queue while the urgent tasks are given higher priority and should be taken earlier than the not-so-urgent ones. This way we can sequence tasks and fulfill priority requirements.

At the project level, some projects have a higher priority than other projects. These projects can be taken earlier than the other projects. So the sequencing of projects can take place similar to what happens in sequencing of orders in manufacturing (see Figures 12.8 and 12.9).

12.4.4 Disassembling

Many orders can contain line items that have different finished products but the raw material or work-in-process material may be the same. For this reason the order line items should be disassembled first to be aggregated later (see Figures 12.10 and 12.11).

Likewise software test projects can be dissected.

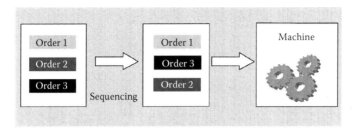

Figure 12.8   Sequencing of orders in manufacturing.

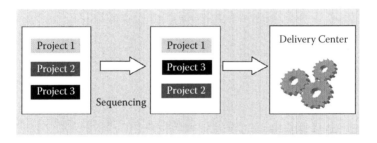

Figure 12.9   Sequencing of projects in software test projects.

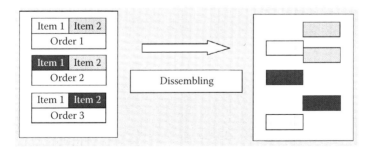

Figure 12.10   Disassembling of orders in manufacturing.

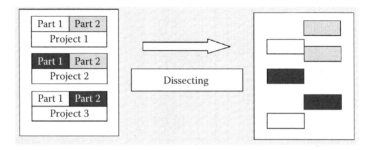

Figure 12.11   Dissection of projects parts in software test project.

12.4.5   Aggregation

At the process steps in manufacturing where the same material is needed for different line items, consolidation of these materials for different orders can be done.

Likewise software test project parts can be consolidated (see Figures 12.12 and 12.13).

12.4.6   Pegging

Each project is broken down into individual tasks. These tasks are assigned to resources belonging to different CoEs. The CoEs may group tasks belonging to different projects so that it may not be possible for an outsider to know exactly which task is being processed currently and which tasks belongs to which project. If these tasks are pegged to the project, then it will be possible for anybody to know to which project the tasks being processed belong (see Figures 12.14 and 12.15).

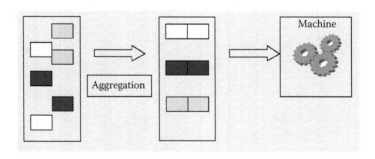

Figure 12.12   Aggregation of line items of orders in manufacturing.

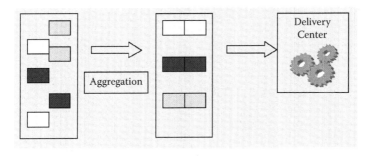

Figure 12.13   Aggregation of project parts of projects in software test projects.

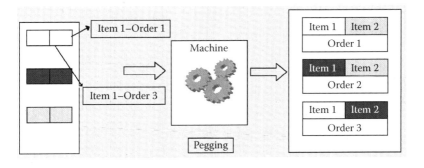

Figure 12.14   Pegging of line items with orders in manufacturing.

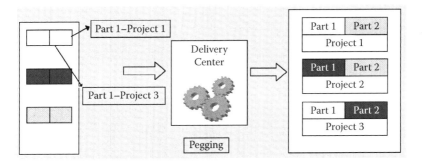

Figure 12.15   Pegging of project parts with projects in software test projects.

12.5   Project versus Manufacturing

Anybody can argue that software development/test engagements are projects. Then how can you think of them as manufacturing activities? After all there is a vast difference between a project and a manufacturing setup!

To elaborate, let us discuss first some concepts in projects and manufacturing and compare the characteristics that make a project a project and a manufacturing process a manufacturing process.

12.5.1   Project

Projects are generally done in longer duration. A project can last from a few days to more than 2 to 3 years. Each project is different from any other project. You form a team to execute a project, and after the project completes, the team is disbanded. For each project, you plan for and procure resources, material, labor, know-how, and so on (see Figure 12.16).

12.5.2   Manufacturing

Products that are being manufactured do not take much time. They may take a few seconds to a few days. Products are manufactured in mass numbers running in sometimes millions per day. Manufacturing processes are repeated continuously. There is no difference between two products if the setup of machines has not changed. Whereas projects can be termed as one of a kind, manufacturing is many of one kind.

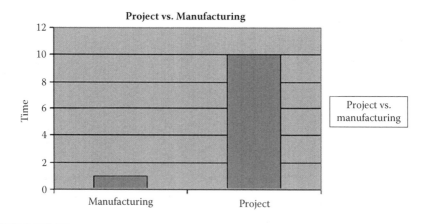

Figure 12.16   Project vs. manufacturing in timescale.

12.5.3   Mass Servicing of Software Test Projects

It might seem antithetical to assume that any software test project can be thought to be similar to any manufacturing activity. They are worlds apart in every aspect. And yet due to some developments in business trends, it could be a reality!

At the service provider's end there are many software test projects going on and coming in all the time. At a big software services provider, more than 20 software test projects might come in each day. That means more than 600 projects per year. In such a scenario it is possible for the service provider to consolidate, disassemble, and aggregate parts of these projects to manage them better. This kind of scenario is required to test our hypothesis of converting projects and apply the mass servicing concept.

The service provider starts by dissecting these projects. Like in manufacturing, he creates an inventory of these project parts. He aggregates similar parts from many projects and puts them into one basket and sends it to the appropriate processing department. This inventory goes through the inventory stages of queued, work-in-process, and finished. The finished parts are then assembled to create finished projects. The service provider then delivers these projects to customers. In essence the projects here do not conform to the dictum "one of a kind" but more closely resemble "many of one kind."

The service provider is using almost the same techniques that a mass manufacturer uses (e.g., pegging, sequencing, disassembling, aggregation, reducing idle and setup time). At his facilities, projects are treated like orders for which processing lines can be set up and project parts can be processed in a mass services manner.

12.5.4   Rework Aspects

In the new setup, will rework increase compared to the existing way of getting work done? Because people working on project parts will not have much of an idea about other parts of the project or the big picture of the project, it is likely that rework may increase as the possibility of error will increase. The better part of this scheme of things is that resources are no longer reporting only to project managers but also to CoE managers. This kind of matrix structure is good, as all to-be-delivered parts are checked from project aspects as well as from technical aspects. So, the chances of doing things wrong will in fact be less.

12.6   Conclusion

Commoditizing test projects can be a great idea. In fact, it can be a revolution. Software vendors can make software that can facilitate test projects to be executed this way. Currently offshore service providers are consolidating test projects. If they can remodel and offer their services this way, they can indeed provide a great value to their customers.

Chapter 13

Quality, Standards, and Software Testing

Many people get confused with software quality, software testing, standards for software development processes, and standards for software product. In fact, many people get confused and use *software testing* and *software quality* interchangeably.

The purpose of writing this book will be defeated until we discuss the relationship between quality, standards, and software testing. Let us discuss these things in detail.

13.1 Quality

Quality in any activity refers to meeting certain norms when the outcome of that activity is measured. A product, when produced, must meet certain physical, aesthetical, chemical, and some other norms set and agreed upon by a certain certifying body to be qualified as a quality product. Only then it is considered appropriate to be consumed by a certain group of people. Now how does a person consider a product suitable for his consumption? He sees the name of the certifying agency on the product label and then decides to consume it or not.

Similarly, when a service is on offer, any person will avail himself of that service only after getting satisfactory information about service quality. And this service quality information is again provided by a certification agency.

A consumer trusts a certifying agency because the certifying agencies are generally unbiased and certify any product or service only after thoroughly testing it and finding that it meets certain standards. If the certifying agency becomes biased and certifies a substandard product or service, then its integrity becomes questionable and the communities where it operates lose faith in it.

Even when the certification process is unbiased, there is a chance of subjective assessment of a product or service attributes against the set norms. For instance, suppose different products (similar but from different manufacturing companies) are being measured for surface finish. The measurement is in terms of coarseness of the surface of the products measured in the number of protruding grains on the surface of the products per square inch. The measuring instruments are the same, but the persons doing the tests are different. When testing is done, there could be two subjective factors: (1) calibration of the testing equipment and (2) ability of the person to measure. So the results for the two products could never be 100% objective, and some element of subjective assessment goes in the measurement.

To reduce this subjective element from the measurement process, the certifying agency must deploy tools and use some standard procedures.

13.2 Standards

For measuring quality of any product or service, we use some standards. For products, it could be physical dimension, chemical composition, or such product attributes. For services, it could be response time, satisfactory resolution of any issue, and so on. We have come to a stage where we can establish product standards that are widely accepted and agreed upon. But in the case of services, standards are still not well defined and are still evolving. Services are intangible and are difficult to measure. A product manufacturer can get away with claims for substandard quality if the law of the land finds that when measured, the product really conformed to the quality standards. But does a service provider have such luck? No way! Conflicts arising out of disputes in service quality cannot be resolved easily, as measuring service quality is very difficult.

As far as commercial activities are concerned, they are immensely influenced by the standards that govern them. Without standards, it will be very difficult to compare any two similar activities and decide which is better in terms of costs, quality, and fulfilling general needs of society. Standards could be in terms of defined methods, specific measurements, defined models, and so on. When standards are in the form of methods or models, they serve as guidelines for performing tasks.

13.2.1 Benchmarking

Even when activities associated with producing goods or providing services are assessed to be conforming to standards, these specific activities may differ from one place to another. The reason is that standards are basically guidelines that are followed when tasks are performed. But implementation of standards will always differ from one place to another. And that is why activities at two places are never the same. This leads to different costs and quality of the product or service provided at these two different places. For instance, primary steel is produced at steel production plants through manufacturing activities. Suppose that at two such plants machines and capacities are the same. But can you say that activities performed at the two plants are exactly the same? No! There will always be some differences that cause costs and quality of the product or service to differ.

For this reason, many businesses resort to benchmarking. A team from one organization visits and observes activities being performed at another organization. This other organization acts as a role model for the first organization. The team from the first organization documents their observations. They come back to their own organization and compare activities performed at their organization to what is being done at the other organization. Later on, they change their own activities and implement what they observed at the other organization. This process is called benchmarking. So effectively they are benchmarking their own activities against the activities being performed at the other organization.

There are many benefits to benchmarking. It can be considered a step above standardization. Definitely benchmarking can provide more value to organizations after they have standardized their processes.

13.2.2 Six Sigma

Six sigma quality methodology was first practiced at Motorola; the quality control department started the initiative to reduce the number of defects in the products by introducing quality control measures in the production process. They identified champions from the people who were working in different process areas in the production process. The task of these champions was to identify problem areas related to quality of the products being produced and take actions to remove these problems. This helped in reducing the number of defects getting introduced in the products. This improved the quality of products and at the same time helped to reduce scrap and rework.

Six sigma methods have been successfully introduced in software development processes.

13.3 Software Development Process Quality

Software development activities are a service. The outcome of software development is a software product or software application. The quality of this application or product can be measured to a large extent (see Figure 13.1).

Before discussing many details of the software development process and its relation to quality, standards, methodologies, and measurements, let us ask some questions:

■ Do we need to measure the software development process?
■ What are the needs of measuring any software development process?

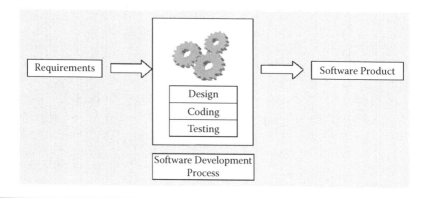

Figure 13.1 Software development process and software product.

- Is any measured software development process better than the one that was not measured?
- How can anybody find out?
- Will two software development processes measured and found to be exactly the same produce software products or applications of the same quality?
- What standards can be set to measure software development process quality?
- Are the standards sufficient to make sure that the produced software will be of good quality?

Now let us find out answers to these questions.

Products are made using machines and product design. Machines are made using machine design. Machine design is conceived and then implemented and the machine is made (see Figure 13.2).

Software is conceived and then developed using a software development process. If the software development process is not sound, then most probably the produced software will not be of good quality. On the other hand, if the software development process can be said to be of good quality, then probably the produced software will be of good quality.

Acknowledging this fact that a good software process will probably produce a better-quality software product, let us see if we can measure quality of software process. But before discussing measures and standards, we must know what is involved in software development. So let us now discuss the steps involved in the software development process.

We can identify that the software development process will have steps like getting requirements, making software design out of these requirements, building software code as per design, and finally testing the built software to know whether it is working as per requirements. We have seen earlier that making a product requires the use of machines. In software product development, where is

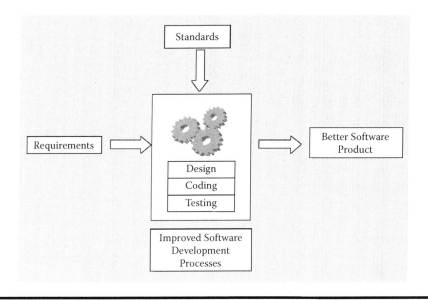

Figure 13.2   Better software processes make better software product.

the machine? Well, the machine is the development infrastructure including programming language and development tools. Software engineers use these to make the software.

Can we measure these processes of requirement gathering, software design, software building, and software testing? Are there any standards that can measure the quality of these processes? What could these standards be?

Before answering these questions, let us now discuss whether the same standards can be applied to all kinds of software development. If not, then are different standards available for measuring different kinds of software? After all, we have software products and applications for many purposes. We have software products to be used by enterprises for business transactions. We have software products for personal use. We have software products for embedded systems. We have software products for managing product development. We have software products to be used by the scientific community. In fact, software is so useful that it is increasingly being used in all aspects of life and every day new areas are discovered to be served by software products and applications.

These software products and applications are of different sizes and types and are used differently. Naturally software processes to make these software products cannot be the same. So can a one-size-fits-all philosophy be applied here? Definitely not! You need different sets of processes to make these different kinds of software products and applications. Although the top-level processes of requirement gathering, software design, software build, and software testing will be the same, the sublevel processes will definitely be different. Many kinds of software are used for mission-critical purposes and many are used casually. The first kind will require stringent quality control measures so that they are defect-free. But the other kind of software product may not need stringent quality control and a certain amount of defects is acceptable.

Let us consider here software products that need to be produced with minimum defects. After all, this book has been written for people who are engaged in making quality software products that have very few defects. In fact, all along we have been discussing how to prevent defects and, after that, how to detect and fix defects that are introduced during software development.

There is one more aspect to software development projects. More and more software development projects are getting outsourced to software services providers. These service providers execute the largest parts of these projects at locations that are far away from customer locations. These locations are based in low-cost countries where cultures are very different from those in the host countries. This poses four challenges: (1) distances, (2) different time zones, (3) geographically scattered teams, and (4) cultural differences. To overcome these barriers, it is very important that everybody involved on the project speak and understand a common language. For this reason there must be a standard process that is followed and understood by all the different people working on the same project but located at different places and having different perceptions.

13.3.1 Standards for Software Development Processes

Now that we have proved the importance of standards in software development processes, let us discuss the standards for software development processes.

One of the best standards for software development processes was developed at the Software Engineering Institute of Carnegie Mellon University. This standard is known as the Capability Maturity Model (CMM). Any organization looking to follow these standards will have to go through a phased approach [1]. These standards are implemented in five distinct phases known as levels. These levels are further divided into what is known as key performance areas (KPAs). Each KPA has some goals known as key performance indicators (KPIs).

Let us discuss these KPAs and KPIs in detail.

13.3.1.1 Requirements

Subprocesses involved in requirements gathering are formulating questionnaire for end users, interviews with end users, documenting the requirements, and so on.

As per CMM methodology, purpose of requirement management is to establish a common understanding between the customer and the software project of the customer's requirements that will be addressed by the software project.

Following are the two KPIs for this area as defined for level 2 maturity in CMM:

1. System requirements allocated to software are controlled to establish a baseline for software engineering and management use.
2. Software plans, products, and activities are kept consistent with the system requirements allocated to software.

13.3.1.2   Software Project Planning

As per CMM methodology, software project planning attempts to establish reasonable plans for performing the software engineering and for managing the software project. There are three KPI goals defined for this area:

1. Software estimates are documented for use in planning and tracking the software project.
2. Software project activities and commitments are planned and documented.
3. Affected groups and individuals agree to their commitments related to the software project.

13.3.1.3   Software Project Tracking and Oversight

The responsibility of software project tracking and oversight is to provide adequate visibility into actual progress so that management can take effective actions when the software project's performance deviates significantly from the software plans.
KPIs are as follows:

1. Actual results and performance are tracked against the software plans.
2. Corrective actions are taken and managed to closure when actual results and performance deviate significantly from the software plans.
3. Changes to software commitments are agreed to by the affected groups and individuals.

13.3.1.4   Software Subcontract Management

The responsibility of software subcontract management is to select qualified software subcontractors and manage them effectively.
The four goals are as follows:

1. The prime contractor selects qualified software subcontractors.
2. The prime contractor and the software subcontractor agree to their commitments to each other.
3. The prime contractor and the software subcontractor maintain ongoing communications.
4. The prime contractor tracks the software subcontractor's actual results and performance against its commitments.

13.3.1.5 Software Quality Assurance

The responsibility of software quality assurance is to provide management with appropriate visibility into the process being used by the software project and of the products being built.

The four goals are as follows:

1. Software quality assurance activities are planned.
2. Adherence of software products and activities to the applicable standards, procedures, and requirements is verified objectively.
3. Affected groups and individuals are informed of software quality assurance activities and results.
4. Noncompliance issues that cannot be resolved within the software project are addressed by senior management.

Apart from these major KPAs, there are many more defined at different levels of CMM. They include software configuration management, process focus, process definition, training, integrated software management, product engineering, defect prevention, technology change management, process change management, quality management, quantitative process management, peer reviews, and intergroup coordination.

As we saw earlier, major software development processes are requirements gathering, software design, software building, and software testing. In the CMM we can see that apart from the requirement-gathering process, other processes are not covered. Actually CMM works as a guideline above these processes and does not specify how to actually perform these processes in a standard manner. In fact, because of this, any organization can develop and implement its own standards to perform activities that come under these process steps and yet claim to be complying with CMM standards, as they are not violating the top-level standards defined by CMM.

Because of this, for software test management, some organizations have come up with a standard known as the Test Maturity Model (TMM).

13.4 Software Testing and Quality

Many people get confused with the difference between software quality assurance and software testing. Let us discuss and clarify this issue.

As has been discussed at length in this chapter regarding what is quality and what are standards, we understand that the quality of a product or a service is the conformance to some standards maintained by certifying agencies. In the case of software development, there will be a quality measurement for the software development process and a quality measurement for the software product or application being produced using the software development process. To make a good-quality software product, the software development process must be of good quality.

So each process activity must conform to some standards so that the overall software development process will have a good quality.

Even after sticking to quality processes, some defects will still exist in the produced software product. Using software testing services, these defects can be detected and then fixed.

So we can conclusively say that quality for a software development process means preventing defects in the software product and software testing means detecting and fixing defects in the software product. Together, these two processes ensure a good-quality software product.

13.5   Quality Standards Evolution

Quality standards, though fairly stable, are prone to change. With increasing sophistication, changing needs of society, and many environmental factors, quality standards keep changing. From the existing standard, new standards keep evolving to keep pace with changing needs. For instance, the Software Engineering Institute at Carnegie Mellon University introduced CMM for software process quality standards. This standard addressed the needs of software development processes. Later people began to feel that software development, software engineering, and software maintenance processes should be governed by a single process standard. So from CMM, a new standard evolved: Capability Maturity Model Integration (CMMI).

In our changing world, nothing is constant. Needs change and so do the processes to fulfill those changed needs. Even the quality standards find it difficult to evolve fast enough so that they can be used to govern the changed processes.

The current business practice of offshoring software testing projects is a good example of how quality standards for processes fall short of meeting changed needs. On the offshored software test projects, the concept of mass servicing is applied. Thus individual software test projects no longer get executed end-to-end by a dedicated project team. Instead parts of the project are executed by different departments of the service provider. At these departments, these projects parts are not treated like projects. Instead they are processed in mass quantities.

This kind of scenario is not covered under any quality standard for software processes. It may take some time before any standards can be devised for these processes.

Bibliography

1. Johnson, D.L. and J.G. Brodman, 2000. Applying CMM Project Planning Practices to Diverse Environments. *IEEE Software*, 17, 4 (July/August), 40–47.

Appendix I

IEEE Standard for Software Test Documentation (ANSI/ IEEE Standard 829-1983)

This is a summary of the ANSI/IEEE Standard 829-1983. It describes a test plan as a document describing the scope, approach, resources, and schedule of intended testing activities. It identifies test items, the features to be tested, the testing tasks, who will do each task, and any risks requiring contingency planning.

This standard specifies the following test plan outline:

Test Plan Identifier

- A unique identifier

Introduction

- Summary of the items and features to be tested
- Need for and history of each item (optional)
- References to related documents such as project authorization, project plan, QA plan, configuration management plan, relevant policies, relevant standards
- References to lower-level test plans

Test Items

- Test items and their version
- Characteristics of their transmittal media
- References to related documents such as requirements specification, design specification, user's guide, operations guide, installation guide
- References to bug reports related to test items
- Items that are specifically not going to be tested (optional)

Features to Be Tested

- All software features and combinations of features to be tested
- References to test design specifications associated with each feature and combination of features

Features Not to Be Tested

- All features and significant combinations of features that will not be tested
- The reasons these features will not be tested

Approach

- Specify the overall approach to testing.
- For each major group of features or combinations of features, specify the approach.
- Specify major activities, techniques, and tools that are to be used to test the groups.
- Specify a minimum degree of comprehensiveness required.
- Identify which techniques will be used to judge comprehensiveness.
- Specify any additional completion criteria.
- Specify techniques that are to be used to trace requirements.
- Identify significant constraints on testing, such as test item availability, testing-resource availability, and deadline.

Item Pass/Fail Criteria

- Specify the criteria to be used to determine whether each test item has passed or failed testing.

Suspension Criteria and Resumption Requirements

- Specify criteria to be used to suspend the testing activity.
- Specify testing activities that must be redone when testing is resumed.

Test Deliverables

- Identify the deliverable documents: test plan, test design specifications, test case specifications, test procedure specifications, test item transmittal reports, test logs, test incident reports, test summary reports.
- Identify test input and output data.
- Identify test tools (optional).

Testing Tasks

- Identify tasks necessary to prepare for and perform testing.
- Identify all task interdependencies.
- Identify any special skills required.

Environmental Needs

- Specify necessary and desired properties of the test environment: physical characteristics of the facilities including hardware, communications and system software, the mode of usage (i.e., stand-alone), and any other software or supplies needed.
- Specify the level of security required.
- Identify special test tools needed.
- Identify any other testing needs.
- Identify the source for all needs that are not currently available.

Responsibilities

- Identify groups responsible for managing, designing, preparing, executing, witnessing, checking, and resolving.
- Identify groups responsible for providing the test items identified in the Test Items section.
- Identify groups responsible for providing the environmental needs identified in the Environmental Needs section.

Staffing and Training Needs

- Specify staffing needs by skill level.
- Identify training options for providing necessary skills.

Schedule

- Specify test milestones.
- Specify all item transmittal events.
- Estimate time required to do each testing task.
- Schedule all testing tasks and test milestones.
- For each testing resource, specify its periods of use.

Risks and Contingencies

- Identify the high-risk assumptions of the test plan.
- Specify contingency plans for each.

Approvals

- Specify the names and titles of all persons who must approve the plan.
- Provide space for signatures and dates.

Appendix II

Software Testing Glossary

This glossary has been made with references and extracts used from the standard glossary of terms used in Software Testing Version 1.2 (dd. June 4, 2006). Produced by the "Glossary Working Party" International Software Testing Qualification Board.

A

Acceptance criteria: The exit criteria that a component or system must satisfy in order to be accepted by a user, customer, or other authorized entity. [IEEE 610]

Acceptance testing: Formal testing with respect to user needs, requirements, and business processes conducted to determine whether or not a system satisfies the acceptance criteria and to enable the user, customers, or other authorized entity to determine whether or not to accept the system. [IEEE 610]

Accessibility testing: Testing to determine the ease by which users with disabilities can use a component or system.

Account: A service provider executes many outsourced projects on behalf of its customers. All projects belonging to one customer are under one account. So each customer is referred by the service provider as one account

Accuracy: The capability of the software product to provide the right or agreed results or effects with the needed degree of precision. [ISO 9126] See also *functionality testing*.

Actual result: The behavior produced/observed when a component or system is tested. Also known as actual outcome.

Ad hoc review: See *informal review*.

Ad hoc testing: Testing carried out informally; no formal test preparation takes place, no recognized test design technique is used, there are no expectations for results, and arbitrariness guides the test execution activity.

Adaptability: The capability of the software product to be adapted for different specified environments without applying actions or means other than those provided for this purpose for the software considered. [ISO 9126] See also *portability.*

Agile testing: Testing practice for a project using agile methodologies, such as extreme programming (XP), treating development as the customer of testing, and emphasizing the test-first design paradigm. See also *test-driven development.*

Algorithm test: See *branch testing.*

Alpha testing: Simulated or actual operational testing by potential users/customers or an independent test team at the developers' site, but outside the development organization. Alpha testing is often employed for off-the-shelf software as a form of internal acceptance testing.

Analyzability: The capability of the software product to be diagnosed for deficiencies or causes of failures in the software, or for the parts to be modified to be identified. [ISO 9126] See also *maintainability.*

Analyzer: See *static analyzer.*

Anomaly: Any condition that deviates from expectation based on requirements specifications, design documents, user documents, standards, and so on, or from someone's perception or experience. Anomalies may be found during, but not limited to, reviewing, testing, analysis, compilation, or use of software products or applicable documentation. [IEEE 1044] See also *defect, deviation, error, fault, failure, incident,* or *problem.*

Arc testing: See *branch testing.*

Attractiveness: The capability of the software product to be attractive to the user. [ISO 9126] See also *usability.*

Audit: An independent evaluation of software products or processes to ascertain compliance to standards, guidelines, specifications, and/or procedures based on objective criteria, including documents that specify the following:

1. The form or content of the products to be produced
2. The process by which the products shall be produced
3. How compliance to standards or guidelines shall be measured. [IEEE 1028]

Audit trail: A path by which the original input to a process (e.g., data) can be traced back through the process, taking the process output as a starting point. This facilitates defect analysis and allows a process audit to be carried out.

Automated testware: Testware used in automated testing, such as tool scripts.

Availability: The degree to which a component or system is operational and accessible when required for use. Often expressed as a percentage. [IEEE 610]

B

Back-to-back testing: Testing in which two or more variants of a component or system are executed with the same inputs, the outputs compared, and analyzed in cases of discrepancies. [IEEE 610]

Baseline: A specification or software product that has been formally reviewed or agreed upon, that thereafter serves as the basis for further development, and that can be changed only through a formal change control process. [IEEE 610]

Basic block: A sequence of one or more consecutive executable statements containing no branches.

Basis test set: A set of test cases derived from the internal structure of a component or specification to ensure that 100% of a specified coverage criterion will be achieved.

Behavior: The response of a component or system to a set of input values and preconditions.

Benchmark test: (1) A standard against which measurements or comparisons can be made. (2) A test that can be used to compare components or systems to each other or to a standard as in (1). [IEEE 610]

Bespoke software: Software developed specifically for a set of users or customers. The opposite is off-the-shelf software. Also known as custom software.

Best practice: A superior method or innovative practice that contributes to the improved performance of an organization under given context, usually recognized as "best" by other peer organizations.

Beta testing: Operational testing by potential and/or existing users/customers at an external site not otherwise involved with the developers, to determine whether or not a component or system satisfies the user/customer needs and fits within the business processes. Beta testing is often employed as a form of external acceptance testing for off-the-shelf software in order to acquire feedback from the market.

Big bang testing: A type of integration testing in which software elements, hardware elements, or both are combined all at once into a component or an overall system, rather than in stages. [IEEE 610] See also *integration testing*.

Black box technique: See *black box test design technique*.

Black box testing: Testing, either functional or nonfunctional, without reference to the internal structure of the component or system.

Black box test design technique: Procedure to derive and/or select test cases based on an analysis of the specification, either functional or nonfunctional, of a component or system without reference to its internal structure.

Blocked test case: A test case that cannot be executed because the preconditions for its execution are not fulfilled.

Bottom-up testing: An incremental approach to integration testing where the lowest-level components are tested first and then used to facilitate the testing of higher-level components. This process is repeated until the component at the top of the hierarchy is tested. See also *integration testing*.

Boundary value: An input value or output value which is on the edge of an equivalence partition or at the smallest incremental distance on either side of an edge, for example the minimum or maximum value of a range.

Boundary value analysis: A black box test design technique in which test cases are designed based on boundary values.

Boundary value coverage: The percentage of boundary values that have been exercised by a test suite.

Boundary value testing: See *boundary value analysis*.

Branch: A basic block that can be selected for execution based on a program construct in which one of two or more alternative program paths are available (e.g., case, jump, go to, if then–else).

Branch condition: See *condition*.

Branch condition combination coverage: See *multiple-condition coverage*.

Branch condition combination testing: See *multiple-condition testing*.

Branch condition coverage: See *condition coverage*.

Branch coverage: The percentage of branches that have been exercised by a test suite. 100% branch coverage implies both 100% decision coverage and 100% statement coverage.

Branch testing: A white box test design technique in which test cases are designed to execute branches.

Bug: See *defect*.

Bug report: See *defect report*.

Business process-based testing: An approach to testing in which test cases are designed based on descriptions and/or knowledge of business processes.

C

Capability Maturity Model (CMM): A five level staged framework that describes the key elements of an effective software process. The Capability Maturity Model covers best practices for planning, engineering, and managing software development and maintenance. [CMM]

Capability Maturity Model Integration (CMMI): A framework that describes the key elements of an effective product development and maintenance process. The Capability Maturity Model Integration covers best practices for planning, engineering, and managing product development and maintenance. CMMI is the designated successor of the CMM. [CMMI]

Capture/playback tool: A type of test execution tool where inputs are recorded during manual testing in order to generate automated test scripts that can be executed later (i.e., replayed). These tools are often used to support automated regression testing.

Capture/replay tool: See *capture/playback tool*.

CASE: Acronym for Computer Aided Software Engineering.

CAST: Acronym for Computer Aided Software Testing. See also *test automation*.

Cause-effect graph: A graphical representation of inputs and/or stimuli (causes) with their associated outputs (effects), which can be used to design test cases.

Cause-effect graphing: A black box test design technique in which test cases are designed from cause-effect graphs. [BS 7925/2]

Cause-effect analysis: See *cause-effect graphing.*

Cause-effect decision table: See *decision table.*

Certification: The process of confirming that a component, system or person complies with its specified requirements (e.g., by passing an exam).

Changeability: The capability of the software product to enable specified modifications to be implemented. [ISO 9126] See also *maintainability.*

Change control: See *configuration control.*

Change control board: See *configuration control board.*

Checker: See *reviewer.*

Classification tree method: A black box test design technique in which test cases, described by means of a classification tree, are designed to execute combinations of representatives of input and/or output domains.

Code: Computer instructions and data definitions expressed in a programming language or in a form output by an assembler, a compiler, or other translator. [IEEE 610]

Code coverage: An analysis method that determines which parts of the software have been executed (covered) by the test suite and which parts have not been executed (e.g., statement coverage, decision coverage, condition coverage).

Code-based testing: See *white box testing.*

Co-existence: The capability of the software product to co-exist with other independent software in a common environment sharing common resources. [ISO 9126] See also *portability.*

Commercial off-the-shelf software: See *off-the-shelf software.*

Compatibility testing: See *interoperability testing.*

Compiler: A software tool that translates programs expressed in a high order language into their machine language equivalents. [IEEE 610]

Complete testing: See *exhaustive testing.*

Completion criteria: See *exit criteria.*

Complexity: The degree to which a component or system has a design and/or internal structure that is difficult to understand, maintain, and verify. See also *cyclomatic complexity.*

Compliance: The capability of the software product to adhere to standards, conventions, or regulations in laws and similar prescriptions. [ISO 9126]

Compliance testing: The process of testing to determine the compliance of the component or system.

Component: A minimal software item that can be tested in isolation.

Component integration testing: Testing performed to expose defects in the interfaces and interaction between integrated components.

Component specification: A description of a component's function in terms of its output values for specified input values under specified conditions, and required nonfunctional behavior (e.g., resource utilization).

Component testing: The testing of individual software components. [IEEE 610]

Compound condition: Two or more single conditions joined by means of a logical operator (AND, OR, or XOR)—for example, A>B AND C>10.

Concrete test case: See *low-level test case.*

Concurrency testing: Testing to determine how the occurrence of two or more activities within the same interval of time, achieved either by interleaving the activities or by simultaneous execution, is handled by the component or system. [IEEE 610]

Condition: A logical expression that can be evaluated as True or False (e.g., A>B). See also *test condition.*

Condition combination coverage: See *multiple-condition coverage.*

Condition combination testing: See *multiple-condition testing.*

Condition coverage: The percentage of condition outcomes that have been exercised by a test suite. 100% condition coverage requires each single condition in every decision statement to be tested as True and False.

Condition determination coverage: The percentage of all single condition outcomes that independently affect a decision outcome that have been exercised by a test case suite. 100% condition determination coverage implies 100% decision condition coverage.

Condition determination testing: A white box test design technique in which test cases are designed to execute single condition outcomes that independently affect a decision outcome.

Condition outcome: The evaluation of a condition to True or False.

Condition testing: A white box test design technique in which test cases are designed to execute condition outcomes.

Confidence test: See *smoke test.*

Configuration: The composition of a component or system as defined by the number, nature, and interconnections of its constituent parts.

Configuration auditing: The function to check on the contents of libraries of configuration items (e.g., for standards compliance). [IEEE 610]

Configuration control: An element of configuration management, consisting of the evaluation, coordination, approval or disapproval, and implementation of changes to configuration items after formal establishment of their configuration identification. [IEEE 610]

Configuration control board (CCB): A group of people responsible for evaluating and approving or disapproving proposed changes to configuration items, and for ensuring implementation of approved changes. [IEEE 610]

Configuration identification: An element of configuration management, consisting of selecting the configuration items for a system and recording their functional and physical characteristics in technical documentation. [IEEE 610]

Configuration item: An aggregation of hardware, software, or both, that is designated for configuration management and treated as a single entity in the configuration management process. [IEEE 610]

Configuration management: A discipline applying technical and administrative direction and surveillance to: identify and document the functional and physical characteristics of a configuration item, control changes to those characteristics, record and report change processing and implementation status, and verify compliance with specified requirements. [IEEE 610]

Configuration management tool: A tool that provides support for the identification and control of configuration items, their status over changes and versions, and the release of baselines consisting of configuration items.

Configuration testing: See *portability testing*.

Confirmation testing: See *retesting*.

Conformance testing: See *compliance testing*.

Consistency: The degree of uniformity, standardization, and freedom from contradiction among the documents or parts of a component or system. [IEEE 610]

Control flow: A sequence of events (paths) in the execution through a component or system.

Control flow graph: A sequence of events (paths) in the execution through a component or system.

Control flow path: See *path*.

Conversion testing: Testing of software used to convert data from existing systems for use in replacement systems.

COTS: Acronym for Commercial Off-The-Shelf software. See *off-the-shelf software*.

Coverage: The degree, expressed as a percentage, to which a specified coverage item has been exercised by a test suite.

Coverage analysis: Measurement of achieved coverage to a specified coverage item during test execution referring to predetermined criteria to determine whether additional testing is required and if so, which test cases are needed.

Coverage item: An entity or property used as a basis for test coverage (e.g., equivalence partitions or code statements).

Coverage tool: A tool that provides objective measures of what structural elements (e.g., statements, branches) have been exercised by a test suite.

Custom software: See *bespoke software*.

Customized software: Changing (adding/deleting/changing) code of a packaged software so that it suits needs of a specific company.

Cyclomatic complexity: The number of independent paths through a program. Cyclomatic complexity is defined as $L - N + 2P$, where

L = the number of edges/links in a graph

N = the number of nodes in a graph

P = the number of disconnected parts of the graph (e.g., a called graph and a subroutine)

Cyclomatic number: See *cyclomatic complexity*.

D

Daily build: A development activity where a complete system is compiled and linked every day (usually overnight), so that a consistent system is available at any time including all the latest changes.

Data definition: An executable statement where a variable is assigned a value.

Data-driven testing: A scripting technique that stores test input and expected results in a table or spreadsheet, so that a single control script can execute all of the tests in the table. Data-driven testing is often used to support the application of test execution tools such as capture/playback tools. See also *keyword-driven testing*.

Data flow: An abstract representation of the sequence and possible changes of the state of data objects, where the state of an object is any of: creation, usage, or destruction.

Data flow analysis: A form of static analysis based on the definition and usage of variables.

Data flow coverage: The percentage of definition-use pairs that have been exercised by a test suite.

Data flow testing: A white box test design technique in which test cases are designed to execute definition and use pairs of variables.

Data integrity testing: See *database integrity testing*.

Database integrity testing: Testing the methods and processes used to access and manage the data(base), to ensure access methods, processes, and data rules function as expected and that during access to the database, data is not corrupted or unexpectedly deleted, updated, or created.

Dead code: See *unreachable code*.

Debugger: See *debugging tool*.

Debugging: The process of finding, analyzing, and removing the causes of failures in software.

Debugging tool: A tool used by programmers to reproduce failures, investigate the state of programs, and find the corresponding defect. Debuggers enable programmers to execute programs step by step, to halt a program at any program statement, and to set and examine program variables.

Decision: A program point at which the control flow has two or more alternative routes. A node with two or more links to separate branches.

Decision condition coverage: The percentage of all condition outcomes and decision outcomes that have been exercised by a test suite. 100% decision condition coverage implies both 100% condition coverage and 100% decision coverage.

Decision condition testing: A white box test design technique in which test cases are designed to execute condition outcomes and decision outcomes.

Decision coverage: The percentage of decision outcomes that have been exercised by a test suite. 100% decision coverage implies both 100% branch coverage and 100% statement coverage.

Decision table: A table showing combinations of inputs and/or stimuli (causes) with their associated outputs and/or actions (effects), which can be used to design test cases.

Decision table testing: A black box test design technique in which test cases are designed to execute the combinations of inputs and/or stimuli (causes) shown in a decision table.

Decision testing: A white box test design technique in which test cases are designed to execute decision outcomes.

Decision outcome: The result of a decision (which therefore determines the branches to be taken).

Defect: A flaw in a component or system that can cause the component or system to fail to perform its required function (e.g., an incorrect statement or data definition). A defect, if encountered during execution, may cause a failure of the component or system.

Defect density: The number of defects identified in a component or system divided by the size of the component or system (expressed in standard measurement terms—for example, lines of code, number of classes, or function points).

Defect Detection Percentage (DDP): the number of defects found by a test phase, divided by the number found by that test phase and any other means afterwards.

Defect management: The process of recognizing, investigating, taking action and disposing of defects. It involves recording defects, classifying them and identifying the impact. [IEEE 1044]

Defect management tool: A tool that facilitates the recording and status tracking of defects. They often have workflow-oriented facilities to track and control the allocation, correction, and retesting of defects and provide reporting facilities. See also *incident management tool*.

Defect masking: An occurrence in which one defect prevents the detection of another. [IEEE 610]

Defect report: A document reporting on any flaw in a component or system that can cause the component or system to fail to perform its required function. [IEEE 829]

Defect tracking tool: See *defect management tool*.

Definition-use pair: The association of the definition of a variable with the use of that variable. Variable uses include computational (e.g., multiplication) or to direct the execution of a path ("predicate" use).

Deliverable: Any (work) product that must be delivered to someone other than the (work) product's author.

Delivery manager: Person who manages outsourced projects from customers from service provider's side. A delivery manager can manage all projects belonging to a specific area (e.g., manufacturing, customer relationship management). Delivery manager is distinct from project managers as he is the single point contact for the customer from service provider's side.

Design-based testing: An approach to testing in which test cases are designed based on the architecture and/or detailed design of a component or system (e.g., tests of interfaces between components or systems).

Desk checking: Testing of software or specification by manual simulation of its execution. See also *static analysis*.

Development testing: Formal or informal testing conducted during the implementation of a component or system, usually in the development environment by developers. [IEEE 610]

Deviation: See *incident*.

Deviation report: See *incident report*.

Dirty testing: See *negative testing*.

Documentation testing: Testing the quality of the documentation (e.g., user guide or installation guide).

Domain: The set from which valid input and/or output values can be selected.

Driver: A software component or test tool that replaces a component that takes care of the control and/or the calling of a component or system.

Dynamic analysis: The process of evaluating behavior (e.g., memory performance, CPU usage) of a system or component during execution. [IEEE 610]

Dynamic analysis tool: A tool that provides run-time information on the state of the software code. These tools are most commonly used to identify unassigned pointers, check pointer arithmetic, monitor the allocation, use, and deallocation of memory, and flag memory leaks.

Dynamic comparison: Comparison of actual and expected results, performed while the software is being executed, for example, by a test execution tool.

Dynamic testing: Testing that involves the execution of the software of a component or system.

E

Efficiency: The capability of the software product to provide appropriate performance, relative to the amount of resources used under stated conditions. [ISO 9126]

Efficiency testing: The process of testing to determine the efficiency of a software product.

Elementary comparison testing: A black box test design technique in which test cases are designed to execute combinations of inputs using the concept of condition determination coverage.

Embedded Software: Software that is made to run with specific electronic devices. This type of software runs only with those devices and may or may not be compatible with other computer systems.

Emulator: A device, computer program, or system that accepts the same inputs and produces the same outputs as a given system. [IEEE 610] See also *simulator*.

Entry criteria: the set of generic and specific conditions for permitting a process to go forward with a defined task (e.g., test phase). The purpose of entry criteria is to prevent a task from starting which would entail more (wasted) effort compared to the effort needed to remove the failed entry criteria.

Entry point: The first executable statement within a component.

Equivalence class: See *equivalence partition*.

Equivalence partition: A portion of an input or output domain for which the behavior of a component or system is assumed to be the same, based on the specification.

Equivalence partition coverage: The percentage of equivalence partitions that have been exercised by a test suite.

Equivalence partitioning: A black box test design technique in which test cases are designed to execute representatives from equivalence partitions. In principle test cases are designed to cover each partition at least once.

Error: A human action that produces an incorrect result. [IEEE 610]

Error guessing: A test design technique where the experience of the tester is used to anticipate what defects might be present in the component or system under test as a result of errors made, and to design tests specifically to expose them.

Error seeding: The process of intentionally adding known defects to those already in the component or system for the purpose of monitoring the rate of detection and removal, and estimating the number of remaining defects. [IEEE 610]

Error tolerance: The ability of a system or component to continue normal operation despite the presence of erroneous inputs. [IEEE 610]

Evaluation: See *testing*.

Exception handling: Behavior of a component or system in response to erroneous input, from either a human user or from another component or system, or to an internal failure.

Executable statement: A statement which, when compiled, is translated into object code, and which will be executed procedurally when the program is running and may perform an action on data.

Execution phase: See also *smoke test*.

Exercised: A program element is said to be exercised by a test case when the input value causes the execution of that element, such as a statement, decision, or other structural element.

Exhaustive testing: A test approach in which the test suite comprises all combinations of input values and preconditions.

Exit criteria: The set of generic and specific conditions, agreed upon with the stakeholders, for permitting a process to be officially completed. The purpose of exit criteria is to prevent a task from being considered completed when there are still outstanding parts of the task which have not been finished. Exit criteria are used to report against and to plan when to stop testing.

Exit point: The last executable statement within a component.

Expected outcome: See *expected result*.

Expected result: The behavior predicted by the specification, or another source, of the component or system under specified conditions.

Experienced-based test design technique: Procedure to derive and/or select test cases based on the tester's experience, knowledge, and intuition.

Exploratory testing: An informal test design technique where the tester actively controls the design of the tests as those tests are performed and uses information gained while testing to design new and better tests.

F

Fail: A test is deemed to fail if its actual result does not match its expected result.

Failure: Deviation of the component or system from its expected delivery, service, or result.

Failure mode: The physical or functional manifestation of a failure. For example, a system in failure mode may be characterized by slow operation, incorrect outputs, or complete termination of execution. [IEEE 610]

Failure Mode and Effect Analysis (FMEA): A systematic approach to risk identification and analysis of identifying possible modes of failure and attempting to prevent their occurrence.

Failure rate: The ratio of the number of failures of a given category to a given unit of measure (e.g., failures per unit of time, failures per number of transactions, failures per number of computer runs). [IEEE 610]

Fault: See *defect*.

Fault density: See *defect density*.

Fault Detection Percentage (FDP): See *Defect Detection Percentage (DDP)*.

Fault masking: See *defect masking*.

Fault tolerance: The capability of the software product to maintain a specified level of performance in cases of software faults (defects) or of infringement of its specified interface. [ISO 9126] See also *reliability*.

Fault tree analysis: A method used to analyze the causes of faults (defects).

Feasible path: A path for which a set of input values and preconditions exists which causes it to be executed.

Feature: An attribute of a component or system specified or implied by requirements documentation (e.g., reliability, usability, or design constraints). [IEEE 1008]

Field testing: See *beta testing*.

Finite state machine: A computational model consisting of a finite number of states and transitions between those states, possibly with accompanying actions. [IEEE 610]

Finite state testing: See *state transition testing*.

Formal review: A review characterized by documented procedures and requirements (e.g., inspection).

Frozen test basis: A test basis document that can only be amended by a formal change control process. See also *baseline*.

Function Point Analysis (FPA): Method aiming to measure the size of the functionality of an information system. The measurement is independent of the technology. This measurement may be used as a basis for the measurement of productivity, the estimation of the needed resources, and project control.

Functional integration: An integration approach that combines the components or systems for the purpose of getting a basic functionality working early. See also *integration testing.*

Functional requirement: A requirement that specifies a function that a component or system must perform. [IEEE 610]

Functional test design technique: Procedure to derive and/or select test cases based on an analysis of the specification of the functionality of a component or system without reference to its internal structure. See also *black box test design technique.*

Functional testing: Testing based on an analysis of the specification of the functionality of a component or system. See also *black box testing.*

Functionality: The capability of the software product to provide functions that meet stated and implied needs when the software is used under specified conditions. [ISO 9126]

Functionality testing: The process of testing to determine the functionality of a software product.

G

Glass box testing: See *white box testing.*

H

Heuristic evaluation: A static usability test technique to determine the compliance of a user interface with recognized usability principles (the so-called heuristics).

High-level test case: A test case without concrete (implementation level) values for input data and expected results. Logical operators are used; instances of the actual values are not yet defined and/or available. See also *low-level test case.*

Horizontal traceability: The tracing of requirements for a test level through the layers of test documentation (e.g., test plan, test design specification, test case specification and test procedure specification, or test script).

I

Impact analysis: The assessment of change to the layers of development documentation, test documentation, and components, in order to implement a given change to specified requirements.

Incident: Any event occurring that requires investigation. [IEEE 1008]

Incident logging: Recording the details of any incident that occurred (e.g., during testing).

Incident management: The process of recognizing, investigating, taking action and disposing of incidents. It involves logging incidents, classifying them and identifying the impact. [IEEE 1044]

Incident management tool: A tool that facilitates the recording and status tracking of incidents. They often have workflow-oriented facilities to track and control the allocation, correction, and retesting of incidents and provide reporting facilities. See also *defect management tool.*

Incident report: A document reporting on any event that occurred (e.g., during the testing) which requires investigation. [IEEE 829]

Incremental development model: A development life cycle where a project is broken into a series of increments, each of which delivers a portion of the functionality in the overall project requirements. The requirements are prioritized and delivered in priority order in the appropriate increment. In some (but not all) versions of this life cycle model, each subproject follows a "mini V-model" with its own design, coding, and testing phases.

Incremental testing: Testing where components or systems are integrated and tested one or some at a time, until all the components or systems are integrated and tested.

Independence: Separation of responsibilities, which encourages the accomplishment of objective testing.

Infeasible path: A path that cannot be exercised by any set of possible input values.

Informal review: A review not based on a formal (documented) procedure.

Input: A variable (whether stored within a component or outside) that is read by a component.

Input domain: The set from which valid input values can be selected. See also *domain.*

Input value: An instance of an input. See also *input.*

Inspection: A type of peer review that relies on visual examination of documents to detect defects (e.g., violations of development standards and nonconformance to higher-level documentation). The most formal review technique and therefore always based on a documented procedure. [IEEE 610, IEEE 1028] See also *peer review.*

Inspection leader: See *moderator.*

Inspector: See *reviewer.*

Installability: The capability of the software product to be installed in a specified environment [ISO 9126]. See also *portability.*

Installability testing: The process of testing the installability of a software product. See also *portability testing.*

Installation guide: Supplied instructions on any suitable media, which guides the installer through the installation process. This may be a manual guide, step-by-step procedure, installation wizard, or any other similar process description.

Installation wizard: Supplied software on any suitable media, which leads the installer through the installation process. It normally runs the installation process, provides feedback on installation results, and prompts for options.

Instrumentation: The insertion of additional code into the program in order to collect information about program behavior during execution (e.g., for measuring code coverage).

Instrumenter: A software tool used to carry out instrumentation.

Intake test: A special instance of a smoke test to decide if the component or system is ready for detailed and further testing. An intake test is typically carried out at the start of the test.

Integration: The process of combining components or systems into larger assemblies.

Integration testing: Testing performed to expose defects in the interfaces and in the interactions between integrated components or systems. See also *component integration testing, system integration testing.*

Integration testing in the large: See *system integration testing.*

Integration testing in the small: See *component integration testing.*

Interface testing: An integration test type that is concerned with testing the interfaces between components or systems.

Interoperability: The capability of the software product to interact with one or more specified components or systems. [ISO 9126] See also *functionality.*

Interoperability testing: The process of testing to determine the interoperability of a software product. See also *functionality testing.*

Invalid testing: Testing using input values that should be rejected by the component or system. See also *error tolerance.*

Isolation testing: Testing of individual components in isolation from surrounding components, with surrounding components being simulated by stubs and drivers, if needed.

Item transmittal report: See *release note.*

Iterative development model: A development life cycle where a project is broken into a usually large number of iterations. An iteration is a complete development loop resulting in a release (internal or external) of an executable product, a subset of the final product under development, which grows from iteration to iteration to become the final product.

K

Key performance indicator: See *performance indicator.*

Keyword-driven testing: A scripting technique that uses data files to contain not only test data and expected results but also keywords related to the application being tested. The keywords are interpreted by special supporting scripts that are called by the control script for the test. See also *data-driven testing.*

L

LCSAJ: A Linear Code Sequence And Jump, consisting of the following three items (conventionally identified by line numbers in a source code listing): the start of the linear sequence of executable statements, the end of the linear sequence, and the target line to which control flow is transferred at the end of the linear sequence.

LCSAJ coverage: The percentage of LCSAJs of a component that have been exercised by a test suite. 100% LCSAJ coverage implies 100% decision coverage.

LCSAJ testing: A white box test design technique in which test cases are designed to execute LCSAJs.

Learnability: The capability of the software product to enable the user to learn its application. [ISO 9126] See also *usability*.

Level test plan: A test plan that typically addresses one test level. See also *test plan*.

Link testing: See *component integration testing*.

Load testing: A test type concerned with measuring the behavior of a component or system with increasing load (e.g., number of parallel users and/or numbers of transactions) to determine what load can be handled by the component or system. See also *stress testing*.

Logic-coverage testing: See *white box testing*.

Logic-driven testing: See *white box testing*.

Logical test case: See *high-level test case*.

Low-level test case: A test case with concrete (implementation level) values for input data and expected results. Logical operators from high-level test cases are replaced by actual values that correspond to the objectives of the logical operators. See also *high-level test case*.

M

Maintainability: The ease with which a software product can be modified to correct defects, modified to meet new requirements, modified to make future maintenance easier, or adapted to a changed environment. [ISO 9126]

Maintainability testing: The process of testing to determine the maintainability of a software product.

Maintenance: Modification of a software product after delivery to correct defects, to improve performance or other attributes, or to adapt the product to a modified environment. [IEEE 1219]

Maintenance testing: Testing the changes to an operational system or the impact of a changed environment to an operational system.

Management review: A systematic evaluation of software acquisition, supply, development, operation, or maintenance process, performed by or on behalf of management that monitors progress, determines the status of plans and schedules, confirms requirements and their system allocation, or evaluates the effectiveness of management approaches to achieve fitness for purpose. [IEEE 610, IEEE 1028]

Master test plan: A test plan that typically addresses multiple test levels. See also *test plan*.

Maturity: (1) The capability of an organization with respect to the effectiveness and efficiency of its processes and work practices. See also *Capability Maturity Model, Test Maturity Model.* (2) The capability of the software product to avoid failure as a result of defects in the software. [ISO 9126] See also *reliability.*

Measure: The number or category assigned to an attribute of an entity by making a measurement. [ISO 14598]

Measurement: The process of assigning a number or category to an entity to describe an attribute of that entity. [ISO 14598]

Measurement scale: A scale that constrains the type of data analysis that can be performed on it. [ISO 14598]

Memory leak: A defect in a program's dynamic store allocation logic that causes it to fail to reclaim memory after it has finished using it, eventually causing the program to fail due to lack of memory.

Metric: A measurement scale and the method used for measurement. [ISO 14598]

Migration testing: See *conversion testing.*

Milestone: A point in time in a project at which defined (intermediate) deliverables and results should be ready.

Mistake: See *error.*

Moderator: The leader and main person responsible for an inspection or other review process.

Modified condition decision coverage: See *condition determination coverage.*

Modified condition decision testing: See *condition determination coverage testing.*

Modified multiple-condition coverage: See *condition determination coverage.*

Modified multiple-condition testing: See *condition determination coverage testing.*

Module: See *component.*

Module testing: See *component testing.*

Monitor: A software tool or hardware device that runs concurrently with the component or system under test and supervises, records, and/or analyzes the behavior of the component or system. [IEEE 610]

Monitoring tool: See *monitor.*

Multiple condition: See *compound condition.*

Multiple-condition coverage: The percentage of combinations of all single condition outcomes within one statement that have been exercised by a test suite. 100% multiple-condition coverage implies 100% condition determination coverage.

Multiple-condition testing: A white box test design technique in which test cases are designed to execute combinations of single condition outcomes (within one statement).

Mutation analysis: A method to determine test suite thoroughness by measuring the extent to which a test suite can discriminate the program from slight variants (mutants) of the program.

Mutation testing: See *back-to-back testing.*

N

N-switch coverage: The percentage of sequences of N+1 transitions that have been exercised by a test suite.

N-switch testing: A form of state transition testing in which test cases are designed to execute all valid sequences of N+1 transitions. See also *state transition testing.*

Negative testing: Tests aimed at showing that a component or system does not work. Negative testing is related to the testers' attitude rather than a specific test approach or test design technique (e.g., testing with invalid input values or exceptions).

Nonconformity: Nonfulfillment of a specified requirement. [ISO 9000]

Nonfunctional requirement: A requirement that does not relate to functionality, but to attributes such as reliability, efficiency, usability, maintainability, and portability.

Nonfunctional testing: Testing the attributes of a component or system that do not relate to functionality (e.g., reliability, efficiency, usability, maintainability, and portability).

Nonfunctional test design techniques: Procedure to derive and/or select test cases for nonfunctional testing based on an analysis of the specification of a component or system without reference to its internal structure. See also *black box test design technique.*

O

Off-shoring: Outsourcing a project and executing it using facilities and resources located at an off-shore location; usually to a low-cost country.

Off-the-shelf software: A software product that is developed for the general market (i.e., for a large number of customers) and that is delivered to many customers in identical format.

Operability: The capability of the software product to enable the user to operate and control it. [ISO 9126] See also *usability.*

Operational environment: Hardware and software products installed at users' or customers' sites where the component or system under test will be used. The software may include operating systems, database management systems, and other applications.

Operational profile testing: Statistical testing using a model of system operations (short duration tasks) and their probability of typical use.

Operational testing: Testing conducted to evaluate a component or system in its operational environment. [IEEE 610]

Oracle: See *test oracle.*

Outcome: See *result.*

Output: A variable (whether stored within a component or outside) that is written by a component.

Output domain: The set from which valid output values can be selected. See also *domain.*

Output value: An instance of an output. See also *output*.

Outsourcer: Company who subcontracts its project to a service provider.

Outsourcing: Subcontracting a project to a service provider who executes the project on behalf of the customer.

P

Pair programming: A software development approach whereby lines of code (production and/or test) of a component are written by two programmers sitting at a single computer. This implicitly means ongoing real-time code reviews are performed.

Pair testing: Two persons (e.g., two testers, a developer and a tester, or an end user and a tester) working together to find defects. Typically, they share one computer and trade control of it while testing.

Partition testing: See *equivalence partitioning*.

Pass: A test is deemed to pass if its actual result matches its expected result.

Pass/fail criteria: Decision rules used to determine whether a test item (function) or feature has passed or failed a test. [IEEE 829]

Path: A sequence of events (e.g., executable statements) of a component or system from an entry point to an exit point.

Path coverage: The percentage of paths that have been exercised by a test suite. 100% path coverage implies 100% LCSAJ coverage.

Path sensitizing: Choosing a set of input values to force the execution of a given path.

Path testing: A white box test design technique in which test cases are designed to execute paths.

Peer review: A review of a software work product by colleagues of the producer of the product for the purpose of identifying defects and improvements. Examples are inspection, technical review, and walkthrough.

Performance: The degree to which a system or component accomplishes its designated functions within given constraints regarding processing time and throughput rate. [IEEE 610] See also *efficiency*.

Performance indicator: A high-level metric of effectiveness and/or efficiency used to guide and control progressive development (e.g., lead-time slip for software development). [CMMI]

Performance testing: The process of testing to determine the performance of a software product. See also *efficiency testing*.

Performance testing tool: A tool to support performance testing that usually has two main facilities: load generation and test transaction measurement. Load generation can simulate either multiple users or high volumes of input data. During execution, response time measurements are taken from selected transactions and these are logged. Performance testing tools normally provide reports based on test logs and graphs of load against response times.

Phase test plan: A test plan that typically addresses one test phase. See also *test plan*.

Portability: The ease with which the software product can be transferred from one hardware or software environment to another. [ISO 9126]

Portability testing: The process of testing to determine the portability of a software product.

Post condition: Environmental and state conditions that must be fulfilled after the execution of a test or test procedure.

Post execution comparison: Comparison of actual and expected results, performed after the software has finished running.

Pre condition: Environmental and state conditions that must be fulfilled before the component or system can be executed with a particular test or test procedure.

Predicted outcome: See *expected result.*

Pretest: See *intake test.*

Priority: The level of (business) importance assigned to an item (e.g., defect).

Probe effect: The effect on the component or system by the measurement instrument when the component or system is being measured (e.g., by a performance testing tool or monitor). For example, performance may be slightly worse when performance-testing tools are being used.

Problem: See *defect.*

Problem management: See *defect management.*

Problem report: See *defect report.*

Process: A set of interrelated activities, which transform inputs into outputs. [ISO 12207]

Process cycle test: A black box test design technique in which test cases are designed to execute business procedures and processes.

Product risk: A risk directly related to the test object. See also *risk.*

Project: A project is a unique set of coordinated and controlled activities with start and finish dates undertaken to achieve an objective conforming to specific requirements, including the constraints of time, cost, and resources. [ISO 9000]

Project risk: A risk related to management and control of the (test) project. See also *risk.*

Program instrumenter: See *instrumenter.*

Program testing: See *component testing.*

Project test plan: See *master test plan.*

Pseudo-random: A series that appears to be random but is in fact generated according to some prearranged sequence.

Q

Quality: The degree to which a component, system, or process meets specified requirements and/or user/customer needs and expectations. [IEEE 610]

Quality assurance: Part of quality management focused on providing confidence that quality requirements will be fulfilled. [ISO 9000]

Quality attribute: A feature or characteristic that affects an item's quality. [IEEE 610]

Quality characteristic: See *quality attribute.*

Quality management: Coordinated activities to direct and control an organization with regard to quality. Direction and control with regard to quality generally includes the establishment of the quality policy and quality objectives, quality planning, quality control, quality assurance, and quality improvement. [ISO 9000]

R

Random testing: A black box test design technique where test cases are selected possibly using a pseudo-random generation algorithm, to match an operational profile. This technique can be used for testing nonfunctional attributes such as reliability and performance.

Recorder: See *scribe.*

Record/playback tool: See *capture/playback tool.*

Recoverability: The capability of the software product to reestablish a specified level of performance and recover the data directly affected in case of failure. [ISO 9126] See also *reliability.*

Recoverability testing: The process of testing to determine the recoverability of a software product. See also *reliability testing.*

Recovery testing: See *recoverability testing.*

Regression testing: Testing of a previously tested program following modification to ensure that defects have not been introduced or uncovered in unchanged areas of the software, as a result of the changes made. It is performed when the software or its environment is changed.

Regulation testing: See *compliance testing.*

Release note: A document identifying test items, their configuration, current status, and other delivery information delivered by development to testing, and possibly other stakeholders, at the start of a test execution phase. [IEEE 829]

Reliability: The ability of the software product to perform its required functions under stated conditions for a specified period of time, or for a specified number of operations. [ISO 9126]

Reliability testing: The process of testing to determine the reliability of a software product.

Replaceability: The capability of the software product to be used in place of another specified software product for the same purpose in the same environment. [ISO 9126] See also *portability.*

Requirement: A condition or capability needed by a user to solve a problem or achieve an objective that must be met or possessed by a system or system component to satisfy a contract, standard, specification, or other formally imposed document. [IEEE 610]

Requirements-based testing: An approach to testing in which test cases are designed based on test objectives and test conditions derived from requirements (e.g., tests that exercise specific functions or probe nonfunctional attributes such as reliability or usability).

Requirements management tool: A tool that supports the recording of requirements, requirements attributes (e.g., priority, knowledge responsible) and annotation, and facilitates traceability through layers of requirements and requirements change management. Some requirements management tools also provide facilities for static analysis, such as consistency checking and violations to predefined requirements rules.

Requirements phase: The period of time in the software life cycle during which the requirements for a software product are defined and documented. [IEEE 610]

Resource utilization: The capability of the software product to use appropriate amounts and types of resources; for example, the amounts of main and secondary memory used by the program and the sizes of required temporary or overflow files, when the software performs its function under stated conditions. [ISO 9126] See also *efficiency*.

Resource utilization testing: The process of testing to determine the resource-utilization of a software product. See also *efficiency testing*.

Result: The consequence/outcome of the execution of a test. It includes outputs to screens, changes to data, reports, and communication messages sent out. See also *actual result, expected result*.

Resumption criteria: The testing activities that must be repeated when testing is restarted after a suspension. [IEEE 829]

Retesting: Testing that runs test cases that failed the last time they were run, in order to verify the success of corrective actions.

Review: An evaluation of a product or project status to ascertain discrepancies from planned results and to recommend improvements. Examples include management review, informal review, technical review, inspection, and walkthrough. [IEEE 1028]

Reviewer: The person involved in the review that identifies and describes anomalies in the product or project under review. Reviewers can be chosen to represent different viewpoints and roles in the review process.

Review tool: A tool that provides support to the review process. Typical features include review planning and tracking support, communication support, collaborative reviews, and a repository for collecting and reporting of metrics.

Risk: A factor that could result in future negative consequences; usually expressed as impact and likelihood.

Risk analysis: The process of assessing identified risks to estimate their impact and probability of occurrence (likelihood).

Risk-based testing: Testing oriented towards exploring and providing information about product risks.

Risk control: The process through which decisions are reached and protective measures are implemented for reducing risks to, or maintaining risks within, specified levels.

Risk identification: The process of identifying risks using techniques such as brainstorming, checklists, and failure history.

Risk management: Systematic application of procedures and practices to the tasks of identifying, analyzing, prioritizing, and controlling risk.

Risk mitigation: See *risk control*.

Robustness: The degree to which a component or system can function correctly in the presence of invalid inputs or stressful environmental conditions. [IEEE 610] See also *error tolerance, fault tolerance*.

Robustness testing: Testing to determine the robustness of the software product.

Root cause: An underlying factor that caused a nonconformance and possibly should be permanently eliminated through process improvement.

S

Safety: The capability of the software product to achieve acceptable levels of risk of harm to people, business, software, property, or the environment in a specified context of use. [ISO 9126]

Safety testing: Testing to determine the safety of a software product.

Sanity test: See *smoke test*.

Scalability: The capability of the software product to be upgraded to accommodate increased loads.

Scalability testing: Testing to determine the scalability of the software product.

Scenario testing: See *use case testing*.

Scribe: The person who records each defect mentioned and any suggestions for process improvement during a review meeting, on a logging form. The scribe has to ensure that the logging form is readable and understandable.

Scripting language: A programming language in which executable test scripts are written, used by a test execution tool (e.g., a capture/playback tool).

Security: Attributes of software products that bear on its ability to prevent unauthorized access, whether accidental or deliberate, to programs and data. [ISO 9126] See also *functionality*.

Security testing: Testing to determine the security of the software product. See also *functionality testing*.

Security testing tool: A tool that provides support for testing security characteristics and vulnerabilities.

Security tool: A tool that supports operational security.

Serviceability testing: See *maintainability testing*.

Service provider: A company who uses its resources to execute outsourced projects from its customers.

Severity: The degree of impact that a defect has on the development or operation of a component or system. [IEEE 610]

Simulation: The representation of selected behavioral characteristics of one physical or abstract system by another system. [ISO 2382/1]

Simulator: A device, computer program, or system used during testing, which behaves or operates like a given system when provided with a set of controlled inputs. [After IEEE 610] See also *emulator.*

Site acceptance testing: Acceptance testing by users/customers at their site, to determine whether or not a component or system satisfies the user/customer needs and fits within the business processes, normally including hardware as well as software.

Smoke test: A subset of all defined/planned test cases that cover the main functionality of a component or system, to ascertain that the most crucial functions of a program work, but not bothering with finer details. A daily build and smoke test is among industry best practices. See also *intake test.*

Software: Computer programs, procedures, and possibly associated documentation and data pertaining to the operation of a computer system. [IEEE 610]

Software feature: See *feature.*

Software quality: The totality of functionality and features of a software product that bear on its ability to satisfy stated or implied needs. [ISO 9126]

Software quality characteristic: See *quality attribute.*

Software Requirement Specification (SRS): For developing any software application for a client, customer requirements are captured and are stored in a document which is commonly known as the SRS document. SRS is primarily divided into 2 parts: functional requirements and non-functional requirements. Functional requirements pertain to requirements which enable the users of the built software to complete their transactions, view reports, and perform other routine tasks. Non-functional requirements are related to performance of the application under different loads on the server on which the application is installed, security, usability, and compatibility. Non-functional requirements are important because they allow the users of the application to complete their tasks using the application without the hindrance of issues related to security, compatibility, and performance.

Software test incident: See *incident.*

Software test incident report: See *incident report.*

Software Usability Measurement Inventory (SUMI): A questionnaire-based usability test technique to evaluate the usability (e.g., user satisfaction) of a component or system.

Source statement: See *statement.*

Specification: A document that specifies, ideally in a complete, precise, and verifiable manner, the requirements, design, behavior, or other characteristics of a component or system, and, often, the procedures for determining whether these provisions have been satisfied. [IEEE 610]

Specification-based testing: See *black box testing.*

Specification-based test design technique: See *black box test design technique.*

Specified input: An input for which the specification predicts a result.

Stability: The capability of the software product to avoid unexpected effects from modifications in the software. [ISO 9126] See also *maintainability.*

Standard software: See *off-the-shelf software.*

Standards testing: See *compliance testing.*

State diagram: A diagram that depicts the states that a component or system can assume, and shows the events or circumstances that cause and/or result from a change from one state to another. [IEEE 610]

State table: A grid showing the resulting transitions for each state combined with each possible event, showing both valid and invalid transitions.

State transition: A transition between two states of a component or system.

State transition testing: A black box test design technique in which test cases are designed to execute valid and invalid state transitions. See also *N-switch testing.*

Statement: An entity in a programming language, which is typically the smallest indivisible unit of execution.

Statement coverage: The percentage of executable statements that have been exercised by a test suite.

Statement testing: A white box test design technique in which test cases are designed to execute statements.

Static analysis: Analysis of software artifacts (e.g., requirements or code) carried out without execution of these software artifacts.

Static analysis tool: See *static analyzer.*

Static analyzer: A tool that carries out static analysis.

Static code analysis: Analysis of source code carried out without execution of that software.

Static code analyzer: A tool that carries out static code analysis. The tool checks source code, for certain properties such as conformance to coding standards, quality metrics, or data flow anomalies.

Static testing: Testing of a component or system at specification or implementation level without execution of that software (e.g., reviews or static code analysis).

Statistical testing: A test design technique in which a model of the statistical distribution of the input is used to construct representative test cases. See also *operational profile testing.*

Status accounting: An element of configuration management, consisting of the recording and reporting of information needed to manage a configuration effectively. This information includes a listing of the approved configuration identification, the status of proposed changes to the configuration, and the implementation status of the approved changes. [IEEE 610]

Status Reporting: Project performance report prepared from time to time, to be sent to customer or stakeholders of a project.

Storage: See *resource utilization.*

Storage testing: See *resource utilization testing.*

Stress testing: Testing conducted to evaluate a system or component at or beyond the limits of its specified requirements. [IEEE 610] See also *load testing.*

Structure-based techniques: See *white box test design technique.*

Structural coverage: Coverage measures based on the internal structure of a component or system.

Structural test design technique: See *white box test design technique.*
Structural testing: See *white box testing.*
Structured walkthrough: See *walkthrough.*
Stub: A skeletal or special-purpose implementation of a software component, used to develop or test a component that calls or is otherwise dependent on it. It replaces a called component. [IEEE 610]
Sub path: A sequence of executable statements within a component.
Suitability: The capability of the software product to provide an appropriate set of functions for specified tasks and user objectives. [ISO 9126] See also *functionality.*
Suspension criteria: The criteria used to (temporarily) stop all or a portion of the testing activities on the test items. [IEEE 829]
Syntax testing: A black box test design technique in which test cases are designed based on the definition of the input domain and/or output domain.
System: A collection of components organized to accomplish a specific function or set of functions. [IEEE 610]
System integration testing: Testing the integration of systems and packages; testing interfaces to external organizations (e.g., Electronic Data Interchange, Internet).
System testing: The process of testing an integrated system to verify that it meets specified requirements.

T

Technical review: A peer group discussion activity that focuses on achieving consensus on the technical approach to be taken. [IEEE 1028] See also *peer review.*
Test: A set of one or more test cases [IEEE 829]
Test approach: The implementation of the test strategy for a specific project. It typically includes the decisions made that follow based on the (test) project's goal and the risk assessment carried out, starting points regarding the test process, the test design techniques to be applied, exit criteria, and test types to be performed.
Test automation: The use of software to perform or support test activities (e.g., test management, test design, test execution, results checking).
Test basis: All documents from which the requirements of a component or system can be inferred. The documentation on which the test cases are based. If a document can be amended only by way of formal amendment procedure, then the test basis is called a frozen test basis.
Test bed: See *test environment.*
Test case: A set of input values, execution preconditions, expected results, and execution post conditions, developed for a particular objective or test condition, such as to exercise a particular program path or to verify compliance with a specific requirement. [IEEE 610]
Test case design technique: See *test design technique.*

Test case specification: A document specifying a set of test cases (objective, inputs, test actions, expected results, and execution preconditions) for a test item. [IEEE 829]

Test case suite: See *test suite.*

Test charter: A statement of test objectives, and possibly test ideas on how to test. Test charters are for example often used in exploratory testing. See also *exploratory testing.*

Test closure: During the test closure phase of a test process data is collected from completed activities to consolidate experience, testware, facts, and numbers. The test closure phase consists of finalizing and archiving the testware and evaluating the test process, including preparation of a test evaluation report. See also *test process.*

Test comparator: A test tool to perform automated test comparison.

Test comparison: The process of identifying differences between the actual results produced by the component or system under test and the expected results for a test. Test comparison can be performed during test execution (dynamic comparison) or after test execution.

Test completion criteria: See *exit criteria.*

Test condition: An item or event of a component or system that could be verified by one or more test cases (e.g., a function, transaction, feature, quality attribute, or structural element).

Test control: A test management task that deals with developing and applying a set of corrective actions to get a test project on track when monitoring shows a deviation from what was planned. See also *test management.*

Test coverage: See *coverage.*

Test cycle: Execution of the test process against a single identifiable release of the test object.

Test data: Data that exists (e.g., in a database) before a test is executed, and that affects or is affected by the component or system under test.

Test data preparation tool: A type of test tool that enables data to be selected from existing databases or created, generated, manipulated, and edited for use in testing.

Test design: See *test design specification.*

Test design specification: A document specifying the test conditions (coverage items) for a test item, the detailed test approach, and identifying the associated high-level test cases. [IEEE 829]

Test design technique: Procedure used to derive and/or select test cases.

Test design tool: A tool that supports the test design activity by generating test inputs from a specification that may be held in a CASE tool repository (e.g., requirements management tool), from specified test conditions held in the tool itself, or from code.

Test driver: See *driver.*

Test-driven development: A way of developing software where the test cases are developed, and often automated, before the software is developed to run those test cases.

Test environment: An environment containing hardware, instrumentation, simulators, software tools, and other support elements needed to conduct a test. [IEEE 610]

Test evaluation report: A document produced at the end of the test process summarizing all testing activities and results. It also contains an evaluation of the test process and lessons learned.

Test execution: The process of running a test on the component or system under test, producing actual result(s).

Test execution automation: The use of software (e.g., capture/playback tools) to control the execution of tests, the comparison of actual results to expected results, the setting up of test preconditions, and other test control and reporting functions.

Test execution phase: The period of time in a software development life cycle during which the components of a software product are executed, and the software product is evaluated to determine whether or not requirements have been satisfied. [IEEE 610]

Test execution schedule: A scheme for the execution of test procedures. The test procedures are included in the test execution schedule in their context and in the order in which they are to be executed.

Test execution technique: The method used to perform the actual test execution, either manually or automated.

Test execution tool: A type of test tool that is able to execute other software using an automated test script (e.g., capture/playback).

Test fail: See *fail*.

Test generator: See *test data preparation tool*.

Test leader: See *test manager*.

Test harness: A test environment comprised of stubs and drivers needed to execute a test.

Test incident: See *incident*.

Test incident report: See *incident report*.

Test infrastructure: The organizational artifacts needed to perform testing, consisting of test environments, test tools, office environment, and procedures.

Test input: The data received from an external source by the test object during test execution. The external source can be hardware, software, or human.

Test item: The individual element to be tested. There usually is one test object and many test items. See also *test object*.

Test item transmittal report: See *release note*.

Test leader: See *test manager*.

Test level: A group of test activities that are organized and managed together. A test level is linked to the responsibilities in a project. Examples of test levels are component test, integration test, system test, and acceptance test.

Test log: A chronological record of relevant details about the execution of tests. [IEEE 829]

Test logging: The process of recording information about tests executed into a test log.

Test manager: The person responsible for project management of testing activities and resources, and evaluation of a test object. The individual who directs, controls, administers, plans, and regulates the evaluation of a test object.

Test management: The planning, estimating, monitoring and control of test activities, typically carried out by a test manager.

Test management tool: A tool that provides support to the test management and control part of a test process. It often has several capabilities, such as testware management, scheduling of tests, the logging of results, progress tracking, incident management, and test reporting.

Test Maturity Model (TMM): A five level staged framework for test process improvement, related to the Capability Maturity Model (CMM) that describes the key elements of an effective test process.

Test monitoring: A test management task that deals with the activities related to periodically checking the status of a test project. Reports are prepared that compare the actuals to that which was planned. See also *test management*.

Test object: The component or system to be tested. See also *test item*.

Test objective: A reason or purpose for designing and executing a test.

Test oracle: A source to determine expected results to compare with the actual result of the software under test. An oracle may be the existing system (for a benchmark), a user manual, or an individual's specialized knowledge, but should not be the code.

Test outcome: See *result*.

Test pass: See *pass*.

Test performance indicator: A high-level metric of effectiveness and/or efficiency used to guide and control progressive test development (e.g., Defect Detection Percentage [DDP]).

Test phase: A distinct set of test activities collected into a manageable phase of a project (e.g., the execution activities of a test level).

Test plan: A document describing the scope, approach, resources, and schedule of intended test activities. It identifies amongst others test items, the features to be tested, the testing tasks, who will do each task, degree of tester independence, the test environment, the test design techniques and entry and exit criteria to be used, and the rationale for their choice, and any risks requiring contingency planning. It is a record of the test planning process. [IEEE 829]

Test planning: The activity of establishing or updating a test plan.

Test policy: A high-level document describing the principles, approach, and major objectives of the organization regarding testing.

Test Point Analysis (TPA): A formula-based test estimation method based on function point analysis.

Test procedure: See *test procedure specification*.

Test procedure specification: A document specifying a sequence of actions for the execution of a test. Also known as test script or manual test script. [IEEE 829]

Test process: The fundamental test process comprises planning, specification, execution, recording, checking for completion, and test closure activities. [BS 7925/2]

Test Process Improvement (TPI): A continuous framework for test process improvement that describes the key elements of an effective test process, especially targeted at system testing and acceptance testing.

Test record: See *test log.*

Test recording: See *test logging.*

Test report: See *test summary report.*

Test reproducibility: An attribute of a test indicating whether the same results are produced each time the test is executed.

Test requirement: See *test condition.*

Test run: Execution of a test on a specific version of the test object.

Test run log: See *test log.*

Test result: See *result.*

Test scenario: See *test procedure specification.*

Test script: Commonly used to refer to a test procedure specification, especially an automated one.

Test set: See *test suite.*

Test situation: See *test condition.*

Test specification: A document that consists of a test design specification, test case specification and/or test procedure specification.

Test specification technique: See *test design technique.*

Test stage: See *test level.*

Test strategy: A high-level description of the test levels to be performed and the testing within those levels for an organization or program (one or more projects).

Test suite: A set of several test cases for a component or system under test, where the postcondition of one test is often used as the precondition for the next one.

Test summary report: A document summarizing testing activities and results. It also contains an evaluation of the corresponding test items against exit criteria. [IEEE 829]

Test target: A set of exit criteria.

Test technique: See *test design technique.*

Test tool: A software product that supports one or more test activities, such as planning and control, specification, building initial files and data, test execution and test analysis. See also *CAST.*

Test type: A group of test activities aimed at testing a component or system focused on a specific test objective (e.g., functional test, usability test, regression test). A test type may take place on one or more test levels or test phases.

Testability: The capability of the software product to enable modified software to be tested. [ISO 9126] See also *maintainability.*

Testability review: A detailed check of the test basis to determine whether the test basis is at an adequate quality level to act as an input document for the test process.

Testable requirements: The degree to which a requirement is stated in terms that permit establishment of test designs (and subsequently test cases) and execution of tests to determine whether the requirements have been met. [IEEE 610]

Tester: A skilled professional who is involved in the testing of a component or system.

Testing: The process consisting of all life cycle activities, both static and dynamic, concerned with planning, preparation, and evaluation of software products and related work products to determine that they satisfy specified requirements, to demonstrate that they are fit for purpose and to detect defects.

Testware: Artifacts produced during the test process required to plan, design, and execute tests, such as documentation, scripts, inputs, expected results, set-up and clear-up procedures, files, databases, environment, and any additional software or utilities used in testing.

Thread testing: A version of component integration testing where the progressive integration of components follows the implementation of subsets of the requirements, as opposed to the integration of components by levels of a hierarchy.

Time behavior: See *performance*.

Top-down testing: An incremental approach to integration testing where the component at the top of the component hierarchy is tested first, with lower-level components being simulated by stubs. Tested components are then used to test lower-level components. The process is repeated until the lowest-level components have been tested. See also *integration testing*.

Traceability: The ability to identify related items in documentation and software, such as requirements with associated tests. See also horizontal traceability, vertical traceability.

U

Understandability: The capability of the software product to enable the user to understand whether the software is suitable, and how it can be used for particular tasks and conditions of use. [ISO 9126] See also *usability*.

Unit: See *component*.

Unit testing: See *component testing*.

Unreachable code: Code that cannot be reached and therefore is impossible to execute.

Usability: The capability of the software to be understood, learned, used, and attractive to the user when used under specified conditions. [ISO 9126]

Usability testing: Testing to determine the extent to which the software product is understood, easy to learn, easy to operate, and attractive to the users under specified conditions. [ISO 9126]

Use case: A sequence of transactions in a dialogue between a user and the system with a tangible result.

Use case testing: A black box test design technique in which test cases are designed to execute user scenarios.

User acceptance testing: See *acceptance testing*.

User scenario testing: See *use case testing*.

User test: A test whereby real-life users are involved to evaluate the usability of a component or system.

V

V-model: A framework to describe the software development life cycle activities from requirements specification to maintenance. The V-model illustrates how testing activities can be integrated into each phase of the software development life cycle.

Validation: Confirmation by examination and through provision of objective evidence that the requirements for a specific intended use or application have been fulfilled. [ISO 9000]

Variable: An element of storage in a computer that is accessible by a software program by referring to it by a name.

Verification: Confirmation by examination and through provision of objective evidence that specified requirements have been fulfilled. [ISO 9000]

Version control: See *configuration control.*

Vertical traceability: The tracing of requirements through the layers of development documentation to components.

Volume testing: Testing where the system is subjected to large volumes of data. See also *resource-utilization testing.*

W

Walkthrough: A step-by-step presentation by the author of a document in order to gather information and to establish a common understanding of its content. [Freedman and Weinberg, IEEE 1028] See also *peer review.*

White box test design technique: Procedure to derive and/or select test cases based on an analysis of the internal structure of a component or system.

White box testing: Testing based on an analysis of the internal structure of the component or system.

Wide Band Delphi: An expert based test estimation technique that aims at making an accurate estimation using the collective wisdom of the team members.

Work around: A technique to find out a way so that the user of any software application which contains a known defect can still use the software application by using the software application in a different way than specified in the user document.

Index